PONS

BEST OF CRIME STORIES

30 Mörderische Kurzkrimis
zum Englischlernen

CONFIDENTIAL

von Dominic Butler

PONS GmbH
Stuttgart

PONS

BEST OF CRIME STORIES

30 Mörderische Kurzkrimis

zum Englischlernen

von Dominic Butler

Alle in diesem Buch geschilderten Handlungen und Personen sind frei erfunden. Ähnlichkeiten mit lebenden oder verstorbenen Personen wären rein zufällig.

PONS verpflichtet sich, den Zugriff auf die zu diesem Buch gehörige Vokabeltrainer-App mindestens bis Ende 2020 zu gewährleisten. Einen Anspruch der Nutzung darüber hinaus gibt es nicht.

1. Auflage 2018

PONS Online-Wörterbuch: www.pons.eu
E-Mail: info@pons.de

Projektleitung: Majka Dischler
Autor: Dominic Butler
Einbandgestaltung: Ilham Widmann
Logoentwurf: Erwin Poell, Heidelberg
Logoüberarbeitung: Sabine Redlin, Ludwigsburg
Layout: Petra Michel, Gestaltung & Typografie, Essen
Satz: Datagroup Int. SRL, Timisoara

ISBN: 978-3-12-562994-3

AUTORENINFO

Dominic Butler

Dominic Butler stammt aus Nordengland. Er ist Englischlehrer und Schriftsteller. Nach seiner Schulzeit, die er an einer klassischen Grammar School (entspricht dem deutschen Gymnasium) verbrachte, studierte er Film und Literatur an der Sheffield Hallam University. Während seiner Studienzeit arbeitete er in Teilzeit als Gerichtsschreiber am Strafgericht in Sheffield. Dort erwachte sein Interesse für Kriminalfälle, die von nun an Thema vieler seiner Kurzgeschichten wurden. Dominic lebt und arbeitet zurzeit in Italien, wo er Englisch unterrichtet und gerade seinen ersten Roman beendet, einen düsteren, jedoch humorvollen Krimi.

EINIGE WORTE VORAB…

Sie lesen gerne Krimis und möchten etwas für Ihr Englisch tun?
Mit diesen spannenden Kurzkrimis frischen Sie Ihr Englisch auf.
Die verwendete Sprache passt genau zum angegebenen Lernniveau
von A2 = leicht (*)
über B1 = mittelschwer (**)
bis zu B2 = schwer (***).
So können Sie den Schwierigkeitsgrad der Geschichten selbst bestimmen und steigern.

Nicht nur Krimis lesen, sondern auch mehr über Land und Leute erfahren:
Im Anschluss an jede Geschichte finden Sie wissenswerte Informationen zu den **Tatorten** und **Schauplätzen**, an denen die Geschichten spielen.

Schwierigere Wörter sind auf jeder Seite in den **Fußnoten** übersetzt. Im Anhang können Sie nochmals alle Wörter in einer alphabetischen **Wortliste** nachschlagen.

Wo die einzelnen Tatorte liegen, können Sie in der **Weltkarte** auf den Seiten 6 und 7 nachschauen.

Alle Wörter, die in den Fußnoten übersetzt sind, können Sie mit der **PONS Vokabeltrainer-App** üben. Gehen Sie einfach auf www.pons.de/kurzkrimis-en und laden Sie die App kostenlos auf Ihr Smartphone oder Tablet herunter!

☠ = Geschichte mit extra Gruselfaktor

INHALTSVERZEICHNIS

	1. MURDER IN THE FOG	*	8
	2. THE LOCH AND THE MONSTER	*	14
☠	3. FOLLOW ME	*	20
	4. THE PERFECT MURDER	*	27
	5. CASE CLOSED	*	34
	6. DON'T MOVE	*	41
	7. ROUTE 66	*	48
	8. THE FALL	*	55
	9. THE OLD SCHOOL TIE	*	62
☠	10. THE TUBE	*	70
☠	11. THE ACCIDENT	**	78
	12. COLD HEART	**	86
	13. THE LOCKED ROOM	**	93
	14. THE HONEY TRAP	**	101
	15. THE MURDER MYSTERY	**	109
☠	16. MURDER IN THE MOONLIGHT	**	117
☠	17. THE END OF THE LINE	**	124
	18. THE FUNERAL	**	131
	19. THE ESCAPE	**	139
☠	20. SIX FEET UNDER	***	147
	21. CAUGHT RED-HANDED	***	154
☠	22. LIKE FATHER, LIKE SON	***	162
	23. MURDER WILL OUT	***	169
	24. MURDER IN THE ICE	***	176
	25. NO SMOKE WITHOUT FIRE	***	184
	26. LITTLE WHITE LIES	***	192
☠	27. WHAT DOES NOT KILL YOU	***	199
☠	28. A SKELETON IN THE CLOSET	***	206
	29. TO DIE FOR	***	213
	30. MURDER IN THE DARKNESS	***	221
	WORTLISTE		235

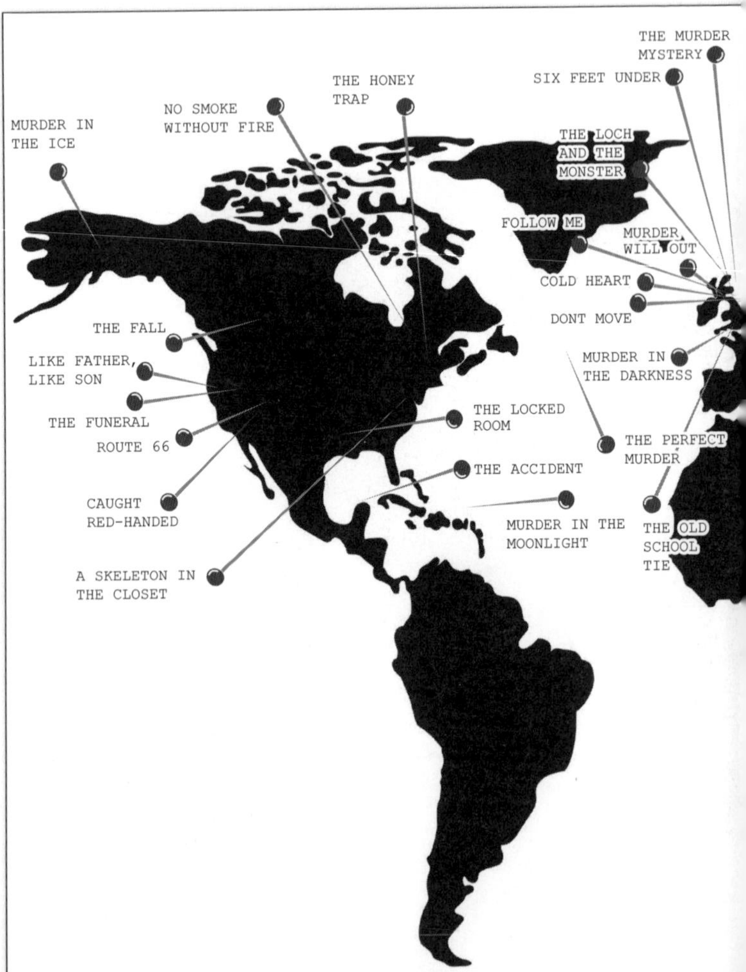
THE MURDER MYSTERY
SIX FEET UNDER
THE HONEY TRAP
NO SMOKE WITHOUT FIRE
MURDER IN THE ICE
THE LOCH AND THE MONSTER
FOLLOW ME
MURDER WILL OUT
COLD HEART
DONT MOVE
THE FALL
LIKE FATHER, LIKE SON
MURDER IN THE DARKNESS
THE FUNERAL
THE LOCKED ROOM
ROUTE 66
THE PERFECT MURDER
THE ACCIDENT
CAUGHT RED-HANDED
MURDER IN THE MOONLIGHT
THE OLD SCHOOL TIE
A SKELETON IN THE CLOSET

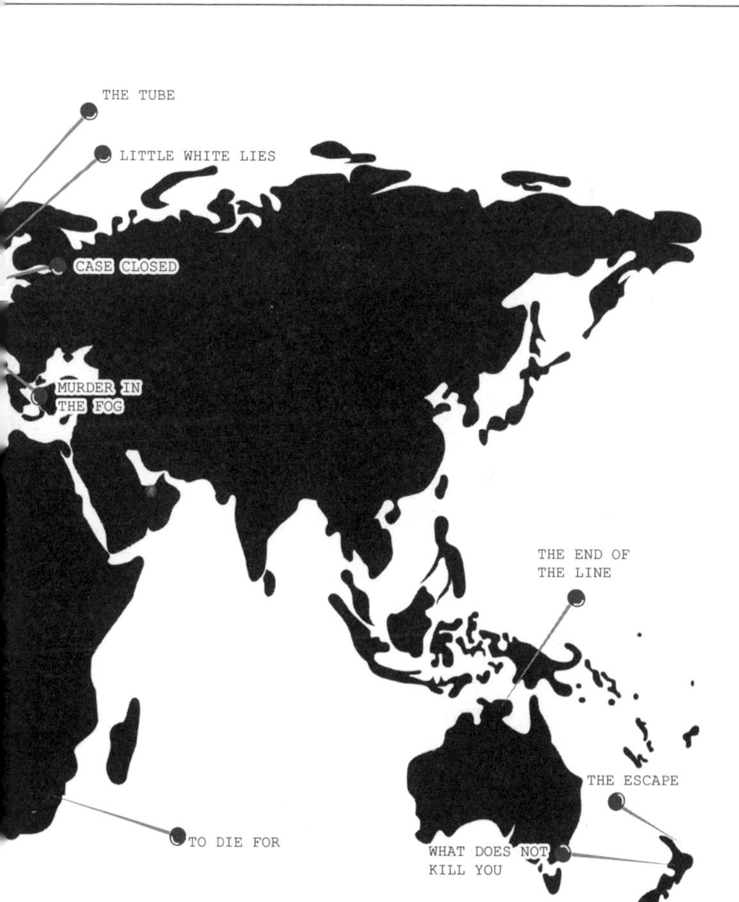

THE TUBE
LITTLE WHITE LIES
CASE CLOSED
MURDER IN
THE FOG
THE END OF
THE LINE
THE ESCAPE
TO DIE FOR
WHAT DOES NOT
KILL YOU

1. MURDER IN THE FOG

I do not remember my name.

This is the first thing that I think when I wake, and I look around nervously, **confused**[1] by the dark and by the thick fog which surrounds me.

I **raise**[2] a hand to my face and feel a short nose and a small mouth. I try to remember my face, I try to remember the colour of my hair or what my eyes look like. I try to remember anything, but I cannot! I have no idea who I am.

I am on the ground **lying**[3] on cold grass which is **wet**[4] from the fog, and I am alone.

Why am I here? I ask myself, but I have no answer. I do not even know where this is because the fog is so thick that I can only see for a few metres in any direction.

I try to stand, but then I **realise**[5] that my head hurts and that there is a **sharp pain**[6] behind my right ear. I carefully lift my hand and touch the large **lump**[7] which is there. It hurts to touch, and I shout in the fog, the sound lost in the dark of the night. When I pull my fingers away, they are wet, and even with no light the blood is bright and easy to see.

I begin to feel more than nervous now: I begin to feel **scared**[8]. I imagine I can see shapes and figures in the fog, and I

1 **confused** – *irritiert*
2 **to raise** – *heben*
3 **to lie** – *liegen*
4 **wet** – *nass*
5 **to realise** – *merken*
6 **sharp pain** – *stechender Schmerz*
7 **lump** – *Beule*
8 **scared** – *verängstigt, ängstlich*

want to run. I feel that I need to run, that there is somewhere I must be, somewhere I must remember.

But before I move, I need to know something. So I push myself up and sit on the ground. I look carefully at my clothes, but they mean nothing. The jeans are new, but now they are dirty: **muddy stains**[1] cover the legs from the wet grass. The t-shirt is not **familiar**[2] either: just simple and black. So I empty my pockets, and at first there is nothing helpful there: no wallet, no keys and no phone. But then I see the **picture**[3], and I stop.

It is a woman, and even in the dark and the fog I recognise her. Her long blonde hair is beautiful, and her kind, friendly, blue eyes are perfect. Yes, I know her! And the thought is so strong that I smile **despite**[4] the pain in the back of my head.

But what is her name? I pull the last item from my pocket. It is a red serviette with a single word written again and again in black **ink**[5].

"Catherine," I say quietly into the fog, and the sound of my voice seems strange and cold.

Catherine. I am sure that I know her, but I still do not remember why. Is she my wife? My girlfriend? I think that she is, and I **suddenly**[6] feel afraid for her. "Catherine!" I shout into the dark, but there is no reply.

I am about to shout again when suddenly I remember something. I remember Catherine's face, but she is not smiling like she is in the picture, and her blue eyes look scared and desperate. I try to remember the image, and I see that there is a

1 **muddy stain** - *Schlammfleck*
2 **familiar** - *vertraut*
3 **picture** - *Foto*
4 **despite** - *trotz*
5 **ink** - *Tinte*
6 **suddenly** - *plötzlich*

piece of cloth[1] in her mouth so that she cannot speak and that she is **tied**[2] **to** a large grey stone by thick white **ropes**[3].

"No!" I **cry out**[4], and I push myself to my feet despite the pain in my head.

I do not know what to do for a moment. I only know that I must find her, that I must help her.

I think about the lump on the back of my head and the fresh blood on my fingers. Is there somebody in the fog? Somebody who has Catherine? Someone who wants to hurt her, who wants to kill her?

I want to shout again, but then I do not. If the person who has Catherine hears me, she is in danger. And another image comes to me. It is the face of a man. An **ordinary**[5] face with small dark eyes and dirty brown hair. There is nothing **cruel**[6] about the face, but I know instantly that this is the man that has Catherine, and I hate that face with all of my heart.

I begin to walk, slowly at first, unsure of the direction that I must go. It seems like the ground is moving slowly up, and I believe that this is right. The image I remember of Catherine tied to the grey stone is in less fog, and I think that it must be on higher ground.

I begin to walk faster, but I am soon running. The fog surrounds me, and the dark is without end. I try not to think of **anything but**[7] the direction I am moving in, but I am starting to remember things now. I remember Catherine. She has a black uniform, which she always wears at work in the restaurant, and on the uniform is a **badge with her name**[8]. "Hello handsome," she always says to me, "another day at the office?" And I never

1 **piece of cloth** - *Stoffstück*
2 **tied to** - *angebunden an*
3 **rope** - *Seil*
4 **to cry out** - *aufschreien*
5 **ordinary** - *herkömmlich, gewöhnlich*
6 **cruel** - *grausam*
7 **anything but** - *nichts anderes als*
8 **badge with her name** - *Namensschild*

say much, but I do not have to: we understand each other without words. And I remember that after I eat, I wait for her in the car park until she finishes work, and she is surprised to see me there. But I **suppose**[1] that's just who I am: a romantic.

Suddenly, there is a sound like a gun shot, and I fall. For a moment I think that I am dead and that Catherine is alone, tied to the grey stone in the fog. But then I see the light in the sky, and I realise that the shot was a **flare**[2]. I watch the light fall and illuminate the **hillside**[3].

Is it the man with the dark eyes and dirty brown hair? Does he know I am here? Good! If he looks for me, he is not with Catherine, I think. And I get up again and run faster now.

Do I hear voices in the fog behind me? I try to turn to look, but the fog behind me is too thick, and I only see the occasional light in the distance.

But in front of me the fog seems to be thinner, and I begin to slow. I am scared now because I know that I am near, and in the dark I begin to see large, grey stones standing like **giants**[4] on the top of the hill. In **amazement**[5], I think that I recognise this circle of ancient stones.

"Stonehenge!" I say.

"Yes," a voice replies, "and this is where it ends." And a tall man steps from behind one of the silent giants.

I **expect**[6] him to have dark eyes and dirty hair, but he does not. His hair is blond, his eyes light, and I think that this is not the man who has Catherine. Maybe he is his friend, his partner, and I am about to run when I see the small gun in his hand.

"I just want Catherine," I say, but I can see the hate in the man's eyes, and I know that the only thing I can do now is run

1 **to suppose** - *vermuten*
2 **flare** - *Leuchtfackel*
3 **hillside** - *Berghang*
4 **giant** - *Riese*
5 **amazement** - *Erstaunen*
6 **to expect** - *erwarten*

to the stone where I know she is tied and try to escape into the fog with her.

"Don't!" says the man, as if he can see my intention in my eyes, but I have to. **At first**[1], I think that maybe I am quick enough, but then I hear the **snap**[2] of the gun and feel the explosion in my back.

For a moment more I run, and I can see the shape of the stone where Catherine is tied, and I fall to the floor in front of it. "Catherine," I shout, but there is no reply. When I look to see why, I see that she is not there: the white ropes are still tied to the stone, but she is not.

"Catherine," I say again, smiling, because **she is all that matters**[3], and I can rest now because I know that she is safe.

"You got him, Detective?" a voice says behind me.

"Yeah, that's him," the tall man says. "He **matches**[4] the girl's description perfectly: dirty brown hair, small dark eyes. And look, the blood behind his ear is where she hit him before she escaped."

"Good for her."

"Yeah. We think she's his third **victim**[5] this year."

"So why didn't he run? Why wait here for us?"

The tall man is silent for a moment: "Who knows? I don't want to understand the mind of these psychopaths. I'm just happy Catherine is okay."

Catherine is okay. Catherine is okay. I do not understand anything else that they say, but I do understand these three words, and I smile again.

Catherine is okay.

1 **at first** - *zuerst*
2 **snap** - *Schuss*
3 **she is all that matters** - *sie ist alles, worauf es mir ankommt*
4 **to match** - *passen*
5 **victim** - *Opfer*

→ **Stonehenge** befindet sich in der Grafschaft Wiltshire im Süden von England und ist wahrscheinlich das berühmteste prähistorische Monument der Welt. Es stammt aus der Zeit zwischen 3000 und 2000 v. Chr., der genaue Entstehungszeitpunkt ist jedoch nicht bekannt. Viele glauben allerdings, dass die Anlage von Anfang an als Begräbnisstätte diente, da zahlreiche verbrannte Menschenreste dort entdeckt wurden. Wegen seiner Verbindung zu heidnischer Magie übt Stonehenge bis zum heutigen Tag eine große Faszination auf viele Menschen aus. Die Entstehung der Steinformation bleibt nach wie vor ein Mysterium.

2. THE LOCH AND THE MONSTER

"No, Darling, she means nothing to me, less than nothing. I hate her. It's only you Emily, I promise... .What? Divorce her? That's impossible... Why? Because of the money, the house, the cars... No, Emily, of course you're more important than them, but... No! No, listen, don't go, listen to me, when I return to London, everything is going to be different... I have a plan, Darling.... Darling, I have a plan... Emily?" But there is no answer, and Oliver Stern puts his mobile back into his coat pocket and looks around.

There is no one near to him to hear. He is alone on the **jetty**[1], apart from the boat **attendant**[2] at his chair twenty metres away, his feet on a boat and a cigarette in his mouth. And he cannot hear from there, Oliver is sure. But just to be safe he decides not to phone Emily again.

Perhaps the less she knows, the better.

A plan. Yes, he has a plan, a good plan, and a simple plan.

He looks out across the horrible, grey **loch**[3]. The sun is almost down behind the green, snowy mountains now, and it is colder than before. "What sort of person wants to have a holiday in this **remote**[4], ugly part of the world?"

Then he hears the sound of his wife's **laughter**[5] from the terrace bar of the hotel, and he **shakes his head**[6].

"The sort of person like my monster of a wife."

1 **jetty** - *Pier*
2 **attendant** - *Wärter*
3 **loch** *(Schottisch)* - *See*
4 **remote** - *abgelegen*
5 **laughter** - *Gelächter*
6 **to shake one's head** - *den Kopf schütteln*

He tries to picture Emily: her eyes are so loving, her laugh so light and pretty. But when his wife laughs, she sounds like a **donkey**[1].

He looks at the loch again, at the jetty and the small boats waiting there for the tourists in the hotel. And he asks himself once more if he can do it.

"Ah ha ha ha ha ha ha ha!" she **brays**[2] again.

And he knows that he can.

It is ten-to-six now; the boats stop going out at six. And the sun is almost gone.

She needs to come now, he knows, but he cannot **shout**[3] for her. No, it is her idea to go on a boat. Everyone in the bar knows she wants to go. I just need to wait for her like a good husband, he thinks.

The type of husband who is happy to go out on the huge, horrible loch, in the dark, with his monster of a wife.

But can she still swim? He is not sure. He thinks that with her clothes and her coat on she will be too heavy and that the cold grey water of the loch will pull her down. But is that **enough**[4]?

He looks at the bag by his feet. The romantic picnic filled with all the food his wife loves. And the bottle of champagne that he knows she cannot resist.

Oliver smiles. It is a heavy bag. All he has to do is make her hold it for a second. Perhaps, quickly **wrap**[5] the **straps**[6] around her hands. Then…

No more monster.

But it is nearly six now.

The attendant is about to finish for the night.

1 **donkey** - *Esel*
2 **to bray** - *wiehern, kreischen*
3 **to shout** - *rufen*
4 **enough** - *genug*
5 **to wrap** - *wickeln*
6 **strap** - *Riemen*

"Excuse me," Oliver shouts with a smile. He pulls his cigarette packet from his pocket and walks over. "Sorry to **bother**[1] you, but do you have a lighter?"

The attendant has a hard face and fierce red hair. He looks at Oliver for a moment, nods, pulls his lighter from his pocket and offers it.

"Look," continues Oliver, "my wife wants to take a boat out. She's going to be here in a second."

The man looks at the sky.

"A boat, man, we want a boat."

"**I dinna ken aboot that. Better the morra.**[2]"

The idiot does not speak English, Oliver thinks. **Bloody**[3] country. "I'm sorry, I don't understand. I'm from England."

The man laughs, stands up and says nothing.

Oliver tries to stay calm, but he knows there is too little time. "Don't you speak English? My wife wants to go out now. **She's only going to be one minute**[4]!" he shouts, and the attendant stops and gives him a long, hard look with his cold, blue eyes.

"Oliver! Here I am!" a loud, cheerful voice says. And the two men turn to see Mrs Sylvia Stern. She smiles that stupid, cow-like smile at them, and Oliver sees the idiot attendant smile back. She is dressed in a horrible **tartan**[5] skirt and woollen jumper. And in her arms she has the heavy wax coat. Good, Oliver thinks.

"Darling," he says, with a smile, "this good man wants to close. I think we must wait until tomorrow now."

"Oh no, surely not?" She turns to the man and smiles again. "Can't we just go out for a few minutes, please? Just to enjoy the sunset?"

1 **to bother** - *stören*
2 **I dinna ken aboot that. Better the morra.** *(Schottisch)* - *Ich weiß nicht. Lieber morgen.*
3 **bloody** *(AUS, BE)* - *verdammt*
4 **She's only going to be one minute.** - *Sie ist gleich da.*
5 **tartan** - *schottengemustert*

And the attendant ignores Oliver but returns her smile. "Ay, well, just for 10 minutes then."

"Oh thank you!" Sylvia says, and the attendant helps them into the small rowing boat and passes Oliver the picnic bag. He then gives him another long, hard look, but Oliver does not care.

"Bloody idiot," he says to Sylvia as they slowly move away from the jetty onto the dark water. "I don't understand a thing he says."

But Sylvia does not **seem**[1] to hear and **instead**[2] looks out at the dark loch.

For five minutes Oliver **rows**[3], and soon the jetty and the hotel look much smaller, while the attendant is almost impossible to see in the half-light of the new evening.

And so this is it.

Oliver thinks about loving, ironic Emily again. Then he looks at his monster of a wife.

Oh yes, this has to be it. No more listening to that awful laugh, no more looking at her boring face. And, perhaps more importantly, no more sharing his bank account with her.

"Darling?" he says. "Shall we have a little drink?"

"Oh yes, that would be very nice!" She smiles, but in the half-light Oliver thinks he sees something strange in her expression.

"Can you pass me over the bag? Then you can come and sit here next to me," he says as casually as he can.

"Of course," Sylvia says, and she stands up, which makes the boat **rock.**[4] Oliver thinks that this is going to be very easy indeed. Just one **push**[5], and then he can shout for the attendant and pretend to help but really just watch the monster go down into the loch.

Just one look back at the jetty to be sure no one can see, he thinks, and he turns his head.

And then it happens.

1 **to seem** - *scheinen*
2 **instead** - *stattdessen*
3 **to row** - *rudern*
4 **to rock** - *schaukeln*
5 **push** - *Stoß, Schubs*

Pain explodes at the back of his head, and his eyes go dark. For a second he does not know where he is. Then he feels hands on him, pushing him and moving him. As he tries to say something, he sees the broken champagne bottle at his feet. Then he falls from the boat, and the ice-cold water takes the words and the air from his mouth.

For a moment he goes down, but then he kicks his legs, and he comes to the surface and looks up at Sylvia in the boat. She has an **oar**[1] in her hands, and she is **reaching it out**[2] to him.

"Yes, closer! Help me!" he shouts, and it is then that he sees the strange expression on her face again. "Sylvia, darling?"

"Don't you dare call me that," she says in a tone as cold as the water. "You're a cheating, lying, horrible monster of a man. You can call that stupid girl of yours 'Darling,' but not me. Never again Oliver Stern, never again."

And then the oar hits him on the head, and he cannot think, and he cannot swim, and the water takes him.

For a few moments he **sinks**[3] slowly into the great loch, but then, somehow, **miraculously**[4], he kicks again, and he comes to the surface once more. Sylvia and the boat are gone, and the half-light is complete **darkness**[5] now. He tries to swim, but his clothes and his coat are too heavy.

The jetty! The attendant! He has to still be there. If he hears me, he can bring a boat out.

"Help me!" he shouts into the darkness. "Help me, for the love of God, help me!"

And on the small jetty on the bank of Loch Ness, the attendant hears, he takes the cigarette from his mouth and smiles. "Sorry, Laddie," he says quietly to the loch. "But I can't understand a word you're saying."

1 **oar** - *Ruder*
2 **to reach sth. out to sb.** - *jdm. etw. hinstrecken*
3 **to sink** - *versinken*
4 **miraculously** - *wie durch ein Wunder*
5 **darkness** - *Dunkelheit*

Loch Ness liegt in den wunderschönen und weit abgelegenen *Highlands*, dem schottischen Hochland, und ist einer der bekanntesten Seen der Welt. Ob sein legendäres Ungeheuer „Nessi" wirklich existiert oder nicht, ist nach wie vor nicht bewiesen.

Was im See bewiesenermaßen lebt, sind unter anderem Lachse, Aale, Elritzen und Forellen. Loch Ness ist zu allen Jahreszeiten sehr kalt. Trotzdem haben einige Schwimmer die Herausforderung angenommen und den See der Länge nach durchquert. Der damals 19-Jährige David Morgan, der heute noch den Rekord hält, schaffte 1983 die doppelte Strecke (74 km) in 23 Stunden und 5 Minuten.

3. FOLLOW ME

"Follow me," says Detective Branwell with a **sigh**[1]. His **shift**[2] finishes in five minutes, but there is no one around in Howarth's quiet police station, and so he leads the woman to the first interview room and tries to **suppress the image**[3] of a pint of beer in the Black Bull pub.

The interview room is cold, the lights weak and grey, but he offers the woman a seat and hopes that this will be quick.

As she takes her coat off, Branwell watches her. She has long brown hair that right now looks a little untidy. And she has deep-green eyes that at the moment are tired and nervous and show something which he does not completely recognise.

"Right," he says, and tries to smile to relax her, "what's all this about, then? The officer at the **front desk**[4] says you need to speak to someone."

"I do," she says, and her voice is thin and tense.

"About what?"

She waits for a moment, uncertain, and then she takes a breath. "About a crime."

Branwell pulls his **notepad**[5] from his pocket and places it in front of him on the table. He has a bad feeling about his pint in the Black Bull pub. "I see," he says, "maybe you can tell me your name first. Your address too."

1 **sigh** - *Seufzen*
2 **shift** - *Schicht*
3 **to suppress the image** - *die Vorstellung unterdrücken*
4 **front desk** - *Empfang*
5 **notepad** - *Notizblock*

She puts her hands on the table, and he sees that her red fingernails are **chipped and bitten**[1]. "Jane Thornton. I live at Brow Top Cottage."

"Brow Top? Oh yes, I remember. You have that little red sports car, don't you?"

"Not now, no," she says, and she picks up her handbag. "Can I smoke?"

"No, sorry **luv**[2]: **rules and regulations**[3]. I can get you a tea if you like," but she shakes her head and puts the bag at her feet. "Then maybe you can tell me why you're here," he **suggests**[4].

Again she waits, and again Branwell thinks that he sees something in her deep-green eyes.

"There's a man who follows me," she begins. "Every evening. Every evening when I return home from work."

Branwell **nods**[5]. "**I see**[6]."

"No you don't. Every evening. Every single evening. For almost a year now. He's always there, Detective. Sometimes he's so close that I think he can touch me, and other times he's far away, but I still know that he's there. And Detective, you might think that I'm crazy, but I know what this man wants…"

"What?" Branwell says. "What does he want?"

She pauses for a second, and he sees her hands shake. "He wants to kill me."

Branwell says nothing but watches the woman's face. She is scared, very scared.

"Does he speak to you, this man?"

"No, never. And when I try to speak to him, he…"

"Yes?"

"He disappears."

1 **chipped and bitten** – *eingerissen und abgekaut*
2 **luv** – *Schatz (Kosename verwendet in Yorskshire auch unter fremden Leuten)*
3 **rules and regulations** – *Regeln und Vorschriften*
4 **to suggest** – *vorschlagen*
5 **to nod** – *mit dem Kopf nicken*
6 **I see.** – *Ich verstehe.*

Branwell opens his notebook and takes his pen out. "Where do you work, Mrs Thornton?"

"Miss Thornton. I work in Leeds. I have a small media company."

"In Leeds? Then where does this man follow you from?"

"From the station at Keighley."

"You work in Leeds, but you don't drive? I think your sports car can get you there a lot faster than the bus to Keighley and then the train to Leeds."

"I told you: I don't drive it. Not now."

"Right, so he follows you..."

"From Keighley. I see him at the train station sometimes; then he's there again when I get off the bus in the town centre here in Howarth. And then he follows me to my cottage."

"You walk from here to Brow Top, up over the **moors**[1] road? Every evening? That's a dangerous road, and it must be more than three miles."

"Dangerous, yes," but she does not say anything else, and Branwell continues.

"Can you describe the man?"

"Easily," she says, but again she pauses, and Branwell sees her turn quickly to look over her shoulder. "He's tall. With dark hair. His skin is **pale**[2] and his eyes cold. Dead," she says. "He has dead eyes. And they watch me every day, and I think that they watch me at night too."

Branwell feels a **shiver**[3] run over his back. "You think that this man enters your **premises**[4]? That he enters your cottage during the night?"

"I do. Sometimes I wake, and I know that he's there. I turn on the lights, and I see nothing, but when I go to the window,

1 **moor** - *Heideland*
2 **pale** - *hell*
3 **shiver** - *Schauder*
4 **premises** *(pl.)* - *Grundstück*

I can see him in the field. He stands there like a **scarecrow**[1] in the dark. And he accuses me... everyday... His cold dead eyes accuse me."

Branwell shakes his head. Is she crazy or just terrified[2]? "Miss Thornton, if this man enters your house, we can arrest him. But to do that we need **evidence**[3]. Has he broken a window? Or **entered the property by force**[4]?"

She lets out a laugh, a laugh that is horrible to Branwell. "No, of course not. There's nothing."

"And he never says anything **threatening**[5]? He never says that he wants to **hurt**[6] you?"

She looks over her shoulder again quickly and automatically as if she does it a hundred times a day. "No, he never says a thing. But I know... I know what he wants. I know what he wants!" And she begins to cry.

Branwell puts the notepad away. "I'm sorry Miss Thornton, but there's very little that we can do. Let me make you that tea. A nice tea to calm you down; then we can start again and see if there are any other details."

She seems to nod, and he stands up and goes to the door. "We need a better description, you see. If we want to identify the man."

"What?" she says before he can open the door. "Oh no, no, you don't understand, Detective. I know who the man is. I know his name. I know everything."

Branwell stops.

"You mean," she continues, "that if I tell you his name, you can help me? You can stop this?" she says **desperately**[7].

1 **scarecrow** - *Vogelscheuche*
2 **to be terrified** - *schreckliche Angst vor etw. haben*
3 **evidence** - *Beweis*
4 **to enter a property by force** - *einbrechen*
5 **threatening** - *bedrohend*
6 **to hurt sb.** - *jdm. wehtun*
7 **desperately** - *verzweifelt*

"You know his name?"

"Do you promise? You can stop it?"

Branwell does not sit. He sees that expression in her eyes again. "I can't promise, luv, no. But I can try."

She nods and bites her red fingernails for a moment. "His name is William Grey."

William Grey. Branwell knows the name. William Grey. And he remembers something horrible from more than a year ago: an accident on the roads across the moors. William Grey: a local cyclist and a good man.

"William Grey? Miss Thornton, William Grey is dead. He was hit by a car last year while he cycled across Brow Top road. We never found the driver, but William died instantly, they say."

"Oh I know," she says, and he sees that something in her deep-green eyes, and he thinks that he knows what it is now. "I know, Detective, because I am that driver."

Then there is only the sound of her crying to fill the cold interview room, and Branwell sits down again and picks up his pen and notepad. "I think you should tell me everything," he says, and he can see clearly now the **guilt**[1] that fills her deep-green eyes.

An hour later Branwell closes the door of the interview room and sighs. He does not **feel any sympathy**[2] for her. He cannot: not for someone who can do that. To leave someone on the grey moors to die. No, he cannot feel any sympathy for her, but maybe now she can find some rest. Maybe now she can forget the ghost of William Grey.

He walks up the corridor to the front desk and **is about to**[3] shout for an officer when he sees the tall figure standing at the door of the police station. He stops, his heart suddenly beating faster.

1 **guilt** - *Schuldgefühl*
2 **to feel sympathy for sb.** - *mit jdm. Mitleid haben*
3 **to be about to do sth.** - *im Begriff sein, etw. zu tun*

The man's dark hair is wet from the rain outside, his skin pale and his eyes cold and dead. It is him. Branwell knows it, but he cannot believe it.

"Do you have her **confession**[1]?" the figure says.

"What?"

"Do you have Miss Thornton's confession?" the figure repeats.

Branwell nods. "Yes. I do. She's in the interview room now."

The figure nods. "Good. Then it's over." And the impossible figure turns to leave.

Branwell still cannot believe it, yet the similarity is perfect. "Wait, Mr Grey, William, wait… I need to ask you…"

But the figure turns and smiles. It is a cold smile, but Branwell sees that the man's eyes look a little more alive now. "My name is Grey, Detective, but not William. My name is Matthew… Matthew Grey. William was my brother…" he says as he opens the door to the rain. "My twin brother."

1 **confession** - *Geständnis*

→ Howarth, ein schöner doch mysteriöser Ort, befindet sich in den **Yorkshire Moors**, dem Heideland der nordenglischen Grafschaft Yorkshire. Die Stadt ist berühmt wegen ihrer Verbindung zu den Brontë Schwestern, die viele ihrer romantischen Romane und Gedichte hier schrieben. Mit ihren Steinstraßen und malerischen Kirchen verzaubert die Stadt all ihre Besucher. Noch mehr wird deren Phantasie jedoch vom Moor angeregt. Meistens ist es in Nebel oder Regen gehüllt und wenn der Wind im Moor sanft zwischen den Bäumen singt, sind es nicht nur die berühmten Schwestern, die sich einbilden Geister zu sehen, die sie aus dem Dunkel beobachten.

4. THE PERFECT MURDER

"The QM2, Darling, is the finest **ocean liner**[1] in the world. Sure, there are one or two bigger than her, but none of them has her romance or her luxury," Mrs Carolina Heath says as they enter the dining room.

Her young, new friend only smiles. She is a quiet young thing, and beautiful too, and Carolina likes to have beautiful things around her, so she is more than happy to talk for both of them.

"This is your first **cruise**[2], you say? You're going to love it. Just look at the view out there." And from the large glass windows they can see the majestic figure of the Statue of Liberty as the ship slowly moves away from the port of New York and heads into the deep of the ocean.

"It's fantastic," Eleanor says, and again Carolina is very happy to have a new **companion**[3].

The dining room is magnificent. The tables are covered in white, and the lights are low and **atmospheric**[4]. The band in the corner is playing soft classical music.

"Well, I wonder what the other people at our table are like. **Oh my**[5], look, here we are, table six. Well, good evening gentlemen." Carolina says, and the three men stop their conversation and smile.

"Mrs Heath," one says, "how good to see you again. Another evening of champagne and dancing?"

1 **ocean liner** - *Ozeandampfer*
2 **cruise** - *Kreuzfahrt*
3 **companion** - *Begleiter(in)*
4 **atmospheric** - *stimmungsvoll*
5 **Oh my!** - *Meine Güte!*

"Every night, Peter. My doctor tells me that I must," she laughs. "Gentlemen, let me introduce you to my new friend Miss Eleanor Chance."

Eleanor only nods and smiles.

"And these, Eleanor, well, how to describe them… I suppose every ship needs some pirates, and these are they. Meet Peter, Edward and Michael."

The men stand and nod politely, and Carolina is amused by the interested looks they give Eleanor Chance.

"Pirates?" Eleanor asks.

"Well, maybe not pirates, but you should still be careful. They are, in fact, writers, and I don't know which is **worse**[1]."

"Writers? How interesting."

"Please, sit down," Edward says with a smile that shows early signs of **infatuation**[2].

"No, I can't, I must find the captain: he promised to tell me all about the new people on board today; you know how I must know who I am sailing with." She looks at the men. "Oh, but can I trust you three to look after Eleanor? This is her first night, and her first cruise. She does not need to hear any of your **horrible**[3] stories or strange ideas."

"Oh, well, **I suppose we can**[4] change the subject, but we are having a really interesting conversation."

Carolina laughs. "I don't want to know! Just be nice." And she smiles at Eleanor. "If they scare you, just scream, and I can **rescue**[5] you."

"Oh, I think I can look after myself," responds Eleanor, and again Carolina thinks what a sweet, lovely thing she is. She must be only twenty-five or twenty-six. Her long blonde hair

1 **worse** - *schlimmer*
2 **infatuation** - *Vernarrtheit*
3 **horrible** - *schrecklich*
4 **I suppose we can...** - *wir können wohl...*
5 **to rescue** - *retten*

is elegant and her face full of classical beauty. And those eyes, such **innocent**[1], blue eyes.

Yes, a lovely, new companion, she thinks as she leaves.

At the table Edward offers Eleanor a chair, and Michael passes her a glass of champagne.

"So, are you all writers?" she asks.

"Yes," says Peter, "of different types. I'm in film, Edward here is a novelist and Michael writes plays."

"Fascinating," she says, and all three look happy that she thinks so.

"And what is this interesting conversation that I am interrupting?"

"Oh, we can't bore you with that. Please, tell us about yourself," says Edward.

Eleanor smiles **shyly**[2] and moves the elegant white silk scarf that lies around her neck above her black dress. "There is very little to say. I am sailing from here to Southampton, then I **intend**[3] to stay in England for some time. For the summer perhaps." Then she is quiet, and the three men think how polite and gentle she seems.

"I see," says Peter. "Well, this is a tradition of ours. Every year we take a cruise on old Mary. This is the sixth year. A good escape from **editors**[4] and deadlines."

"And wives," says Michael.

"Well, for them, not for me: I'm not married," says Edward a little too quickly.

For a moment there is an **awkward silence**[5], and Peter and Michael exchange a smile.

"Well, our conversation is about murder," says Peter to fill the silence "the perfect murder."

Eleanor smiles. "I see."

1 **innocent** - *unschuldig*
2 **shyly** - *schüchtern*
3 **to intend to** - *beabsichtigen*
4 **editor** - *Herausgeber(in); Redakteur(in)*
5 **awkward silence** - *betretenes Schweigen*

"I'm sure she's not interested, Pete," says Edward.

"Oh, but I am. Mrs Heath is lovely, but she only talks about scandal and **gossip**[1]."

"See, Edward, we can continue to argue!" Michael jokes. "You see, we all have very different ideas about what the perfect murder is. Peter thinks that for a film there must be something visual about the murder **weapon**[2]. For me the important things are the character and the motive."

"And for me," Edward says as he **refills**[3] Eleanor's glass, "the important thing is the **twist**[4]."

"The twist?"

"You know, the surprise at the end of the story, the thing you don't expect."

Eleanor smiles and takes a drink. The Statue of Liberty is still visible in the distance, but they will soon be alone on the dark ocean.

"You know, I think you're all correct. In fact, I have an idea for a story: an idea I think about **occasionally**[5]."

"Really?" says Peter, "Well you must tell us."

"Maybe," she says with another shy smile, "but you first: what's your idea for the perfect murder weapon?"

Peter laughs. "Okay, well, it's not my idea, and it's old, but I think it's great for a film. It's an **icicle**[6]."

The other two men laugh. "He always says this," Edward informs Eleanor.

"Because it's perfect. After the murderer kills the victim, they just watch the weapon melt. No fingerprints, no **evidence**[7]. What do you think, Eleanor?"

1 **gossip** - *Tratsch*
2 **weapon** - *Waffe*
3 **to refill sb.'s glass** - *jdm. nachschenken*
4 **twist** - *Wendung*
5 **occasionally** - *gelegentlich*
6 **icicle** - *Eiszapfen*
7 **evidence** - *Beweis*

She smiles, "It's very clever... but... well, I prefer fire."

"Fire?"

"Yes, fire kills, and it **destroys**[1] the evidence. And also a fire can look like an accident. The icicle never can."

"Ha, she's right!" laughs Michael. "So what about characters and motive?" he continues.

"A beautiful, young couple who are happy and in love."

"What, and he kills her?"

"No, she kills him."

"Let me guess: they're rich, she wants his money?"

Eleanor takes another drink. "No. She's the rich one."

"So what's the motive?" Michael asks.

"Wait a minute," interrupts Peter. "You say she kills him. With fire? How? She locks him in a room in a burning house?"

"No, because then he might escape. She drugs him with **sleeping pills**[2] during dinner. She always goes for a run in the evening, but this time she waits until he falls asleep in a chair in the lounge, and she puts a candle to the curtains. Then she goes for her run and makes sure that many people see her."

Peter nods his head, "Interesting, but a **coroner**[3] will find **traces**[4] of sleeping pills in the blood. They'll know."

"No, not with this type of pill. At a certain temperature it completely burns away. Only a small trace of it can be **detected**[5]. And if they are detected, **so what**[6]? They are his pills."

Peter laughs this time. "Excellent!"

"Very clever," Edward agrees, "but unfortunately the wife is always a **suspect**[7] in a murder."

1 **to destroy** - *vernichten*
2 **sleeping pill** - *Schlaftablette*
3 **coroner** - *Gerichtsmediziner*
4 **trace** - *Spur*
5 **to detect** - *entdecken*
6 **So what?** - *Na und?*
7 **suspect** - *Verdächtige(r)*

"Normally, yes," says Eleanor, and all three men notice how her smile **fades**[1] a little, "but she has a plan for that. You see, she runs until she hears the **fire engines**[2]. Then she returns to the house. There are people there already, neighbours, and this is just what she wants. They try to stop her, but she runs into the burning building. No one follows her. They can't: they know it's too dangerous. And so she goes to her husband as the flames **spread**[3] over his body, and she watches. And while she watches, she lets the flames touch her, too. They reach out, and they burn her back and her neck and her hair. And at this point she screams and runs from the building and falls to the floor." Eleanor stops speaking, and for a moment there is silence at the table.

"My God," says Edward, "she lets the flames burn her."

Michael takes a moment to think about it and then nods. "It's perfect. The perfect way to avoid **suspicion**[4]."

"Everyone thinks it's an accident and that she is **heartbroken**[5]," says Peter.

"Yes," Eleanor says, and for a moment more there is silence again.

Then the band starts to play a waltz, and Eleanor looks at Edward. "I don't suppose you dance, Edward?"

And the writer goes a little red. "Actually, I do. Would you like to join me?"

Eleanor smiles, and they both stand up. She **adjusts**[6] the white scarf around her neck.

"But what about the woman's motive?" Michael asks.

Eleanor smiles. "Yes, that's the difficult part. And I'm afraid I just don't know. I suppose sometimes a person just… enjoys murder."

1 **to fade** - *schwinden*
2 **fire engine** - *Feuerwehrauto*
3 **to spread** - *sich ausbreiten*
4 **suspicion** - *Verdacht*
5 **heartbroken** - *untröstlich*
6 **to adjust** - *zurechtrücken*

And as Eleanor and Edward move away to the dance floor, Peter and Michael see her adjust the scarf around her neck one last time. And in the low, romantic light of the ballroom they both think they see something strange on her back and neck. Something which makes them stop and look at each other.

But no, it cannot be what they think it is.

It cannot be burnt skin under the elegant white scarf.

Can it?

Die **QM2, Queen Mary the Second**, ist der einzige transatlantische Ozeandampfer, der derzeit die Reise von Southampton nach New York antritt. Diese Reise führt über den oft stürmischen Nordatlantik - die gleiche Strecke, auf der einst die "unsinkbare" Titanic ihr Ende fand.

Die QM2 ist ein luxuriöses und romantisches Schiff, mit dem schon Adlige, Prominente und einige der reichsten und erfolgreichsten Persönlichkeiten der Welt gereist sind. Natürlich sind auch einfachere Menschen willkommen, die nicht im Rampenlicht stehen und dieses wunderbare, meisterhafte Schiff genießen möchten.

5. CASE CLOSED

Normally Nick likes his job, but not today. Today he just wants to get out of the hot **courtroom**[1], away from the serious lawyers in their black **gowns**[2] and white **wigs**[3] and go and enjoy the sun.

It is a good job, he thinks. It is better than serving drinks in a pub or helping out at his dad's office, but only if it is a short day, and only if the case is closed quickly. But today it is nearly three, and the case is **nowhere near closed**[4].

Still, he likes the title of his job. "Court reporter" sounds good; it sounds important, and that is exactly how he describes it to any girl that asks. In reality, however, all he does is press 'play' on the **recording device**[5] and write down a few notes about when the judge enters, when the **prosecution**[6] or **defence**[7] speaks, or what the final **verdict**[8] is.

And sometimes the cases are interesting, and he likes having some good stories to tell the guys in the pub. He also enjoys deciding who is innocent and who is guilty, but today that is too easy.

So he looks out of the window and waits for the judge. Sometimes he looks across at the **defendant's**[9] sister, a young woman with long, dark hair and sad eyes. But only sometimes, because the defendant and the rest of her family, the Lee family,

1 **courtroom** - *Gerichtssaal*
2 **gown** - *Talar*
3 **wig** - *Perücke*
4 **nowhere near closed** - *längst nicht abgeschlossen*
5 **recording device** - *Aufnahmegerät*
6 **prosecution** - *Staatsanwaltschaft*
7 **defence** - *Verteidigung*
8 **verdict** - *Urteilsspruch*
9 **defendant** - *Angeklagte(r)*

are wild, and he does not want to make her, or them, angry. They have a **terrible reputation**[1] in Bristol, and there is not one of them that does not scare Nick.

"**All rise!**[2]" the **court clerk**[3] says, and the jury, the lawyers and the family of the defendant all stand. Nick does too, and he remembers to press the button on the device. He forgot to do it once, and they refused to pay him for the day.

"Please be seated!" says the judge, a woman of about forty years of age with a serious face and tone. "My summary of this case is **brief**[4]. The jury knows all the details. On Wednesday the fifth of January Mrs Dawson went to the house of her sister, the defendant, Miss Lee. Mrs Dawson was bleeding from her nose and mouth; she also had marks on her face. She says her husband, the **deceased**[5] Mr Dawson, hit[6] her there several times. There are pictures of these **injuries**[7], but there is no proof that Mr Dawson hit Mrs Dawson. However, that is not why you are here. You are here because when Miss Lee saw her younger sister, she took a **pair of scissors**[8] from her kitchen table, said something to her sister and left the house. The words she said were 'I will kill him,' but the defendant says she does not remember that. Several people saw the defendant walking around Bristol looking for Mr Dawson. She stopped twice: once at the house of one of Mrs Dawson's friends and once at a local pub. Both times she had the scissors with her, and both times witnesses **testified**[9] that she said 'I will kill him.'

At half past two in the afternoon on the fifth of January Miss Stella Lee found Mr Dawson. He was leaving a cafe with

1 **terrible reputation** - *schlechter Ruf*
2 **All rise!** - *Bitte erheben Sie sich!*
3 **court clerk** - *Gerichtsdiener*
4 **brief** - *kurz*
5 **deceased** - *verstorben*
6 **to hit** - *schlagen*
7 **injury** - *Verletzung*
8 **a pair of scissors** - *eine Schere*
9 **to testify** - *aussagen*

a friend. The friend, Mr Harris, says that Miss Lee did not say anything to Mr Dawson and that the only thing Mr Dawson said was 'Hello'. Miss Lee then **stabbed**[1] Mr Dawson in the neck with the scissors, and he died in seconds **due to**[2] loss of blood. Miss Lee waited until the police came and was arrested.

Ladies and gentleman of the jury, you must decide only one thing. The defence says that this is not murder, but **manslaughter**[3]. They say this is the case because Miss Lee was not **in a sane state of mind**[4] when she killed Mr Dawson; they say that this crime was in defence of her sister. The prosecution says this is not true. They say this is **premeditated murder**[5] because for half an hour Miss Lee looked for Mr Dawson; they also say she made her intention clear on three different occasions. Please, leave us now, and take some time to consider these events."

"All rise!" the court clerk says again. The judge leaves, the jury returns to its room to make a verdict, and the Lee family exit to wait in the lobby.

Nick sighs. It is obvious what the decision will be, but it looks like he will be here until four now. Cigarette time then, he thinks, and he leaves the courtroom. He has at least ten minutes; no jury can make a decision in less than ten minutes.

He takes the back stairs, passes three or four lawyers in their black gowns and white wigs and feels sorry for them: it is so hot today. Then he pushes open a fire door to his personal smoking area at the back of the court next to the bins and lights his cigarette.

The feeling of the sun on his face is good, and the taste of the smoke is even better. Tonight is a good night to go out for a few drinks, he thinks, and he is deciding whom to call, when

1 **to stab sb.** – *jdn. niederstechen*
2 **due to** – *infolge*
3 **manslaughter** – *Totschlag*
4 **in a sane state of mind** – *zurechnungsfähig*
5 **premeditated murder** – *vorsätzlicher Mord*

he hears a female voice.

"Yeah, everything is fine, perfect... no, no one has an idea. Not the police, not my **mental**[1] family... of course it will be murder... What? Oh, who cares about her? She'll probably like prison, the **crazy**[2] cow: more people for her to hurt. And then I get his money, and you and I can **get the hell out of this city**[3] and out of this country."

Nick walks to the bins and looks around them; on the other side is the sister of the defendant. In the court room she always looks sad and confused. Now, however, she looks only **victorious**[4].

"Jesus," Nick says before he can stop himself, and the girl sees him and closes the mobile phone in her hand.

Nick looks at her for a second and then turns and runs back to the door.

He walks back up the stairs feeling confused and uncertain. He has to say something to someone, but who? The judge? Maybe.

He pushes the door to the courtroom open. No one is there. He moves towards another door and then hears someone else enter court.

"Wait," Mrs Dawson says, and she looks like she might cry. "Please wait: I need to explain."

Nick waits. Why not? What can she do to him in here?

She stands near to him, and he can see the tears in her eyes and the sad expression on her face, but this time he knows it is not real.

"I heard you. Your own sister? You wanted her to kill your husband."

1 **mental** - *übergeschnappt*
2 **crazy** - *verrückt*
3 **to get the hell out of this city** - *aus dieser Stadt abhauen*
4 **victorious** - *siegreich*

"No, you don't understand. I don't know what you heard, but I love my sister, and I used to love my husband."

For a second only Nick waits. Then he shakes his head and **is about to**[1] turn.

"Look," she says, her voice different now, "I saw you looking at me yesterday. Maybe there is something we can do to make you forget this? Maybe you can take me for a drink." Then she smiles and takes his hand. For a second he does not know what to say, but he knows what to do, and he pulls his hand away and moves to the door.

For a second she is silent, but then she speaks again, though this time her voice is hard and angry. "Fine, go and tell them what you heard. Do you have any proof? No. So you can tell them what you want, but they can do nothing, and you are still here in Bristol, and so is my family. And they will not like what you say. Do you understand me?"

Nick stops. He understands, and she is right: there is nothing he can do.

"That's right, little boy. Keep quiet and you are going to be okay. I never hurt anyone; she did. Is it my fault she is so stupid? So easy to manipulate? A little bit of blood on my face, a few tears, a **fake**[2] story about him hitting me. It was so easy. And if you tell anyone, it is going to be just as easy to finish you. Understand?"

Then the door opens and the lawyers return, and Mrs Dawson's expression of sadness returns. Slowly they all come back in, and Nick knows he has to say something. He has to do something.

But there is no time, and there is nothing he can do. The Lee family is back in the room now, and he looks at them. They are **savage**[3], terrible people, who love violence.

1 **to be about to do sth.** - *im Begriff sein, etw. zu tun*
2 **fake** - *falsch*
3 **savage** - *brutal*

So, he moves back to his desk, and he sits down in the seat and feels **defeated**[1].

He wants to say something, but without proof he has nothing, and the judge can do nothing.

And he hears the door to the judge's **chamber**[2] open.

"All rise!" and Nick knows it is too late now.

He stands and is about to press the button on the recording device when he sees the red light flashing.

The red light?

The red light means it is recording.

It is recording…

It was recording…

It recorded…

"Stop!" Nick shouts, and he hands the recording device to the court clerk. "I think the judge needs to listen to this first," he says, and he looks back at the beautiful Mrs Dawson and sees that she is not sad now, and that she is not victorious, and not angry.

And he smiles at her because he thinks this expression **suits**[3] her best.

Yes, he thinks Mrs Dawson looks best when she is scared.

1 **defeated** - *besiegt*
2 **chamber** - *Amtskammer*
3 **to suit sb.** - *jdm. stehen*

→ Die klassischen Merkmale des **britischen Justizsystems** sind in der ganzen Welt bekannt: Weiße Perücken und schwarze Talare, ernstblickende Richter und Geschworene, die im Gerichtssaal sitzen, sind typisch für Großbritannien.

Basis des britischen Rechtssystems ist das Common Law, das auch in Australien, U.S.A. und Kanada angewendet wird. Das Common Law unterscheidet sich vom Civil Law, das in Kontinentaleuropa angewendet wird, hauptsächlich darin, dass es auf der Basis von richterlichen Urteilen immer weiterentwickelt wird. Auf vergangene richterliche Urteile, die sogenannten Präzedenzfälle, kann man sich für aktuelle Urteile berufen.

6. DON'T MOVE!

It feels like[1] ice-cold water.

One moment you are **asleep**[2], your dreams calm and gentle and your body warm in the blankets of your bed. The next moment you are **awake**[3], a horrible **sensation**[4] filling your body, and you are sure that ice-cold water is covering you.

But it is not.

No, it is something much worse. Something that makes your heart beat faster. Something that **makes the hairs on your arms stand up**[5] and that makes your eyes search the horrible, complete darkness of your room.

No, it is not ice-cold water: it is **fear**[6].

And for a few moments you are so afraid that you cannot think. You know you are still in your bed, still in your house, still in your quiet street in the north of Manchester. And you want to tell yourself to relax, that everything is okay, and to close your eyes and return to your calm and gentle dreams.

But you cannot.

No, you cannot, because you know that everything is not okay. You know that you are awake because something woke you.

Some noise. Some movement. *Somebody.*

And you try to remember what it was, but you cannot.

1 **It feels like...** - *Es fühlt sich an wie...*
2 **to be asleep** - *schlafen*
3 **awake** - *munter*
4 **sensation** - *Gefühl*
5 **to make sb.'s hair stand up** - *jdm. die Haare zu Berge stehen lassen*
6 **fear** - *Angst*

So, you **lie**[1] there, and, you let your eyes **adjust**[2] to the dark. And you do not tell yourself to relax, you do not tell yourself that everything is okay, and you do not tell yourself to return to your calm and gentle dreams.

You tell yourself this: don't move!

The blanket of your bed is covering all of you **except for**[3] your head, and part of you thinks that this is good. Part of you wants to cover your head too. To hide, to be completely silent and to wait.

But another part of you wants to know.

Needs to know.

So you listen, and you look, and you try to remember what it was that woke you. A dog outside in the street? The alarm of a car? A baby crying in the next house?

Or something closer? Something inside the house? The sound of breaking glass? The **noise**[4] of the front door opening? A voice in the dark?

So you do not move, but you let your eyes adjust, and soon the complete darkness is not so complete. And you can see your room now, **though**[5] everything seems strange and different, and everything makes you feel more afraid.

The door of your **wardrobe**[6] is open, and the clothes inside look like three or four small **burglars**[7] watching you. The lamp in the corner of the room looks like the tall, silent **figure**[8] of a murderer, and the coat on the back of your door has hands that almost touch you.

But this is just your imagination, your fear, and you know that and try to stay calm and focussed.

1 **to lie** - *liegen*
2 **to adjust to** - *sich an etw. gewöhnen*
3 **except for** - *bis auf*
4 **noise** - *Geräusch*
5 **though** - *jedoch*
6 **wardrobe** - *Kleiderschrank*
7 **burglar** - *Einbrecher(in)*
8 **figure** - *Gestalt*

So you listen, and you think that everything seems to be normal. Inside the room everything is silent, apart from the slow and constant tick of the small clock on the wall, and the fast, irregular beat of your heart.

You try to see the clock in the dark, but it is impossible, and you think that it must be somewhere between four and six o'clock: the darkest hours of the night when even the lively and **vibrant**[1] city of Manchester sleeps.

Yes, outside the house the streets are silent. There are no shouts or loud voices coming from university students returning home from the pubs and bars. There is not yet the sound of the milk **van**[2] or **rubbish collectors**[3]. And there is no birdsong to let you know that the sun and the new day are nearly here.

You can imagine the street outside: twenty **terraced houses**[4] stretching down the road. Small houses, with **neither** rich **nor**[5] poor people inside them. All with tidy and ordinary gardens and ordinary cars. All silent and all dark.

You think that if you scream, someone will hear you.

But you are not sure. Not completely sure.

And so you wait, and you listen, and you look, and you tell yourself one more time...

Don't move!

After a few more moments, you begin to feel a little more relaxed. The street is silent and the house is too. Maybe it was only a bad dream that woke you. Maybe it was a text on your mobile phone. Maybe it was an animal in the garden.

And then you think of Sophie, your cat. But you know that the noise was not her. You know that Sophie is sleeping in her usual position at the top of the stairs and that she never makes a noise in the night, and you wish, for the first time, that you

1 **vibrant** - *lebendig*
2 **van** - *Lieferwagen*
3 **rubbish collector** - *Müllabfuhr(wagen)*
4 **terraced house** - *Reihenhaus*
5 **neither... nor** - *weder... noch*

also had a dog. A large **brave**[1] dog to bark and **growl**[2] at any **intruders**[3]. Yes, a brave dog to protect you instead of just a **lazy**[4] cat that lies in dangerous places.

And you almost smile, and you relax a little more.

It was just a bad dream, you think. And your heart slows, and the sensation of ice-cold fear begins to leave you.

And now you move. You pull the covers down to your **chest**[5] and make yourself comfortable again. And you know that you can rest now: everything is okay. And your eyes close, and you feel sleep begin to take you.

And then you hear it!

There! A sound! Not a dream, but movement in the **spare room**[6], where you keep the computer!

Don't move! Part of you says, the part that feels the sensation of cold water on your skin again.

But there is another part of you now, and it is not cold with fear: it is hot. Hot with anger. Because you know now that someone is in your house.

A burglar! Someone is here to steal your things!

Don't move! Part of you says again.

But you do.

Quietly, you move the blankets from your body, and you take the **dressing gown**[7] from the end of your bed and put it on. You know you should call the police, but you need to do something more, something quick.

At the side of your bed, there is a table, and on the table there is a small statue. It is a statue of a woman, and it is your favourite statue.

1 **brave** - *mutig*
2 **to growl** - *anknurren*
3 **intruder** - *Einbrecher(in)*
4 **lazy** - *faul*
5 **chest** - *Brust*
6 **spare room** - *Gästezimmer*
7 **dressing gown** - *Bademantel*

It is also a very heavy statue.

You pick it up, hold it like a **club**[1] and **swing**[2] it.

Yes, it is heavy enough. One hit to the head.

But can you do it? Can you hit someone? Can you hit a burglar?

Then you hear another noise from the spare room.

My computer, you think. My new computer.

And then you know that yes, you can do it if you need to. **If you have to**[3]. If there is someone in the next room trying to steal your new computer. Someone who thinks they can enter your house in the middle of the night!

What if there are two people? Two burglars? Or three?

Don't move! The **scared**[4] part of you says.

But you must. You walk silently to the door of your room. You quietly open it, just a little, just so you can see the dark **landing**[5].

Now you can hear the movement more easily. There are no voices. No reason for you to think that there is more than one burglar. You open the door a little more and step out onto the landing. It is colder here, but you do not feel it. Your heart is beating so fast that you do not feel anything but the strange mixture of fear and anger.

You move quietly, your back to the wall. The light switch is not near your door but halfway to the stairs. The door to the spare room is half open, and you can hear the sound of the wind outside. You know now that the window to the spare room is open, and you know this is how the burglar entered.

You take one more step to the door. Your hand is nearly on the light switch when you hear another noise from the room. Then the door begins to open slowly and quietly. You want to

1 **club** - *Knüppel*
2 **to swing** - *schwingen*
3 **If you have to.** - *Wenn du musst.*
4 **scared** - *verängstigt*
5 **landing** - *Treppenabsatz*

turn back and run to your room and hide under the blanket and be completely silent and not move.

But this is your house, and you know you must stay!

Then, standing right in front of you in the dark, you see the burglar, and he looks back at you and shouts. You turn on the lights and swing the heavy statue in his direction, but you cannot see him now because the light is so bright. You hear your new computer fall to the floor and break, and the burglar shouts again.

And then you can see his face, and you **realise**[1] that he looks more afraid than you do, and he is stepping quickly backwards to the stairs. He is young: just a kid, just a stupid kid…

Then you see Sophie, in her normal place at the top of the stairs, and you see how near the burglar is. You only have time to shout two words…

"Don't move!"

But it is too late, and he does move…

And then he falls.

1 **to realise** - *feststellen*

→ Im 19. Jahrhundert begann **Manchester** sich explosionsartig zu vergrößern, vor allem aufgrund der Textilindustrie. Diese erlebte mit der industriellen Revolution einen Boom und machte Manchester zur ersten industrialisierten Stadt der Welt.

Daher ist es kein Zufall, dass ausgerechnet Manchester der Geburtsort der Suffragetten-Bewegung (der Frauenbewegung, die für das Frauenwahlrecht kämpfte) innerhalb des Vereinigten Königreichs war und dass Karl Marx und Friedrich Engels hier begonnen haben, das Kommunistische Manifest zu schreiben.

Manchester ist heute eine der wirtschaftsstärksten Regionen Großbritanniens und gemessen am Bruttosozialprodukt belegt es hinter London und Birmingham den dritten Platz in England.

7. ROUTE 66

The car is big and old, but it is a classic, and it moves along the road like a **shark**[1], the evening sun reflecting off the red **paint**[2].

The roof is down, and Dan enjoys the feeling of the wind in his hair. It cools him and helps him to **stay awake**[3]. He is tired, very tired, and he still feels sick from the beer and whiskey of last night.

Soon he can stop, find a quiet area off the road and push back the chair and sleep. But not yet: the Mojave Desert is still all around him with its flat orange sands and dead bushes. The plan was to get to Flagstaff, but it is too many miles away. So instead he just wants to get as far from the town called Needles as he can before the night comes.

Needles. He hates that town.

And that girl.

He looks at his right hand on the **steering wheel**[4]. The skin is **raw**[5], and he tries to remember exactly what happened last night, but he cannot. And maybe he should not.

Stupid girl.

But anyway, why think about it? Just drive; get a few more miles from the town, and from her.

He hits the button for the radio, and an old song fills the silence of the desert. A good song, he thinks; a real song. All guitars and rock and roll. He feels a little better. Maybe it is time for the first drink of the day after all, and he takes the small

1 **shark** - *Hai*
2 **paint** - *Lack*
3 **to stay awake** - *munter bleiben*
4 **steering wheel** - *Lenkrad*
5 **raw** - *wund*

flask[1] from the pocket of his denim jacket, removes the lid and **swallows**[2].

For a second the taste is **foul**[3]. A horrible reminder of last night, of the girl and of the hotel room. But then the hot whiskey starts to fill him, and he smiles, puts his head back and laughs loudly into the desert.

"Route Sixty-Six!" he shouts, and he turns the volume of the radio up. He can forget about last night, about the girl. His shirt has a little blood on it, and his hand **is sore**[4]. But he can get a new shirt, and the whiskey will help the pain.

No, this is his holiday, his escape from all those idiots back in California. Forget Needles and forget the girl. Just relax and enjoy it. She was not the first girl, and he knows she will not be the last.

Maybe there is one waiting for him in Flagstaff. And this one, he hopes, will have a little more respect for him and won't laugh at him.

So he drives, and for a while he feels better. The sun is lower in the sky now, it's a little less hot, and the radio keeps him company with old songs about love and women, rock and roll and country music. Real music.

But then the songs stop, and the news report starts. There's something about Needles, something about trouble on Route Sixty-Six, and he tries to listen, but **the signal is weak**[5].

"... a young... dead... the police are looking... a man, probably alone, and thought to be extremely dangerous... any information call..." and then the signal fails, and there is only the sound of the old classic engine and the silence of the desert.

"Dead? No, no it can't be her!"

1 **flask** - *Flachmann*
2 **to swallow** - *schlucken*
3 **foul** - *grauenhaft*
4 **to be sore** - *weh tun*
5 **the signal is weak** - *der Empfang ist schlecht*

He looks at his hand again and tries to **make a fist**[1], but it hurts.

And he thinks of the white shirt in the **trunk**[2] of the car: the white shirt with blood on it.

What did he do last night? He tries to remember, he tries to remember exactly what happened. He remembers the bar clearly. He remembers buying her a drink and then another and another. He remembers that afterwards they were in the hotel room kissing, but then something happened, and she laughed. She **laughed at him**[3], but he cannot remember why. It was something stupid: something he said or did.

And then…

But the rest is impossible to remember. He woke up late in the hotel room and was alone. He saw the blood, but there was only a little, and his hand hurt. And he knew.

Yeah, he could not remember, but he knew.

And he thinks of all the times he watched his father hit his mother.

"Jesus!" he says, and he does not feel tired anymore. He puts his foot on the **accelerator**[4], and the car starts to speed along the old road. Forget sleeping, forget Flagstaff. He needs to find another route and a motel to stay in for a few days: a cheap motel where they only want a name and some cash.

The sun is almost down now, the sky a deep orange and red. And the road is empty.

Or it is until he speeds past the large **billboard**[5]. Then suddenly the road is not empty: there is a car behind him. Its red and blue lights fill the evening, and the sound of the siren fills his ears.

1 **to make a fist** - *eine Faust machen*
2 **trunk** *(AE)* - *Kofferraum*
3 **to laugh at sb.** - *jdn. auslachen*
4 **accelerator** - *Gaspedal*
5 **billboard** - *Reklametafel*

"No!" he **groans**[1] as he sees it in the mirror. And he thinks for a moment about not stopping, but there is nowhere for him to go. "Jesus, just **stay cool**[2], Dan, just stay cool," he tries to tell himself as the red car slows down. So he stops on the **edge**[3] of the desert, hides the flask of whiskey under the seat and lights a cigarette to cover the smell.

God, he wishes he could remember last night: not just the girl's **expression**[4] when he hit her, but everything.

In the mirror he sees the **cop**[5] car park behind him, and he watches a young, tall cop get out.

Just one. Good. If things get serious, then maybe he can manage if there is just one.

He watches the cop walk slowly to the car. The guy's eyes are covered by silver sunglasses, and there is something strange about his uniform, Dan thinks. But before he can decide what, the cop is at the door, and Dan drops his cigarette.

"Evening, officer," he says, and tries to look sorry. "I know I was going a little too fast. I'm sorry."

The cop looks at him and nods, but says nothing. Dan wants to see the eyes behind the glasses but cannot.

"I suppose it's this road: the desert makes it easy to forget to watch your speed," he says, and he thinks he sees the cop look at his hand.

Jesus, is this it? Did he really do something to that girl? More than hit her once? Did he do what they said on the radio? Was she dead?

"Yep," the cop says, "these roads are funny like that. Lots of people have problems out here. This is a nice car. A classic. Yours?" And his voice is slow.

1 **to groan** - *stöhnen*
2 **to stay cool** - *ruhig bleiben*
3 **edge** - *Rand*
4 **expression** - *Gesichtsausdruck*
5 **cop** *(AE, ugs.)* - *Bulle*

"Yes, sir. I have my **licence**[1] here and the **registration**[2]."

The cop nods but does not take them. "I need to ask you to get out of the car."

Dan tries to smile. "Is there a problem, officer?" And he looks at the gun on the cop's belt. If he can get the gun, then he can escape. Forget California. Go north, to Canada, or Alaska.

But he waits. Maybe this is something else, a **routine check**[3], a formality. Be cool, Dan, he tells himself.

"Just get out of the car please," the cop repeats.

Dan nods and gets out, and he thinks again that there is something strange about the cop's uniform. It's small, too small for a tall man like him.

"I need to see in the trunk of the car, sir."

Jesus, the shirt, the shirt is in the trunk. Is that what he wants? "The trunk? Can I ask why?"

"Just routine."

Just routine? Maybe it is, and the shirt is in his bag, at the bottom where it cannot be seen. "Okay."

He walks around to the trunk, the cop behind him, and he pushes the button. For a moment he does nothing. He remembers the **baseball bat**[4] he keeps in there. If the cop asks to look in his bag, he can reach in, **grab**[5] the bat and **take a swing**[6]...

Maybe it can work.

"Sir?" the cop says.

"Sure," and Dan starts to lift the lid of the trunk. But in the reflection of the red paint he sees the cop raise his hand, and in the soft evening light he sees the knife, and for a moment he does not understand.

1 **licence** - *Führerschein*
2 **registration** - *Kraftfahrzeugbrief*
3 **routine check** - *Routinekontrolle*
4 **baseball bat** - *Baseballschläger*
5 **to grab** - *sich etw. schnappen*
6 **to take a swing** - *nach jdm. schlagen*

But then he moves. He is almost quick enough, but the knife still cuts him, and he screams and falls to the floor. The cop falls too, and there is a moment of confusion, but then Dan pushes himself up onto his feet and runs. He sees the cop car and runs to it and pulls open the door.

That's when he sees the **bodies**[1]. One is clearly a policewoman, but the other, a short man, has no uniform.

"Jesus!" he screams, and he remembers the news story on the radio.

"A young... dead... the police are looking... a man, probably alone, and thought to be **extremely**[2] dangerous... any information call..."

And he starts to run again, not on the road now, but into the desert. He wants to turn to look back to see if the man is following him, but he does not **dare**[3]. He thinks that if he keeps running he can escape and find help; find the real police.

But the sun is gone now, and darkness is all around him. Now everything from last night is coming back to him. He remembers hitting the girl, he remembers her shouting at him and he remembers telling her to get out.

And he remembers the last thing she said before she closed the door to the hotel room.

"I hope you die and **rot**[4] in the desert!" she shouted, blood still on her face.

And he almost laughs **in disbelief**[5].

But then he hears someone running behind him, and he screams instead.

1 **body** - *Leiche*
2 **extremely** - *äußerst*
3 **to dare** - *wagen*
4 **to rot** - *verfaulen*
5 **in disbelief** - *ungläubig*

→ Die **Route 66**, die sich von Chicago (Illinois) bis nach Santa Monica (Kalifornien) quer durch Amerika über 3.939 Kilometer zieht, ist eine der berühmtesten Straßen der Welt und das Traumziel vieler Motorradfahrer. Die Strecke zwischen Needles (Kalifornien) und Flagstaff (Arizona), die durch die staubige Wüste führt, ist sehr einsam und hat dadurch nicht nur etwas Romantisches, sondern auch etwas Gefährliches an sich.

Als einspurige und in vielen Strecken kurvenreiche Landstraße konnte die Route 66 schon in den 1950er Jahren nicht mehr Schritt mit dem modernen wachsenden Straßenverkehr halten. Ihr wurden immer öfter die Fernstraßen vorgezogen, die in jenen Jahren massiv ausgebaut wurden.

8. THE FALL

Brandon tries not to think as he walks through the snow that **reaches up**[1] to his **waist**[2].

He is confused and **weak**[3].

He tries not to remember the expression on Greg's face as the bullet hit him in the back.

"You said it was easy!" Brandon calls out into the forest of silent trees that **surround**[4] him, his voice full of emotion. "You said no one could **get hurt**[5]!"

But someone did get hurt.

And now Brandon is alone, and he feels tired and lost, and he knows that the man in the dark winter coat and black hat is near. And he thinks that the next bullet is for him.

He tries to move faster through the snow, but it is so deep… and it is so cold. His clothes are wet and his skin frozen. He wants to put his hand in his coat pocket, but he has to keep the grey pistol ready.

He remembers the way that Greg fell. One moment they were running; the next there was the sound of the gun and a scream. Then Greg was on the floor; Brandon wanted to stop and help him, but Greg told him to run. To **escape**[6] and to not say anything to anyone. And then Brandon heard another gunshot, so he ran and left his brother in the snow to die alone.

1 **to reach up to** - *bis... hinaufreichen*
2 **waist** - *Taille*
3 **weak** - *schwach*
4 **to surround** - *umgeben*
5 **to get hurt** - *verletzt werden*
6 **to escape** - *fliehen*

"You said it was easy!" he shouts again and **recalls**[1] the first time his brother had told him about the plan.

"Listen to me," his brother said at a dark table in the corner at the Lake Louise Inn. "It's easy, Bran. I know exactly what to do."

Brandon put his beer down. "But a kid? Greg, I don't want to **hurt**[2] a kid."

"What?" his brother said, his eyes full of anger: "You think I do? Idiot, we won't hurt anyone. We just take the kid in the truck. Then we phone the hotel. We tell them to tell the parents they can have the kid when they leave us the money. It's easy. No one can get hurt."

But Brandon was not so sure. He knew his brother was a criminal. He knew that he **brewed**[3] illegal beer to sell and that he drove drugs across Alberta and British Colombia. But Brandon did not do that. He did not do any of that. He worked in the **lumber yard**[4], and he tried to do things right. He tried to be better than that.

But now...

"Brandon," his brother said, "I know you need the money. You don't have a job. Your truck is in pieces. You can't find work if you can't drive. What does Sally say?"

Brandon shook his head. "Sally **left**[5] me last month," he said, and he called the waiter for another beer. "Tell me again. Tell me everything again."

Now, alone in the forest, he thinks he can hear the sound of feet in the snow behind him, and he tries to move faster.

There is another sound too. A sound that he recognises; a sound that is getting nearer. It is like constant **thunder**[6] in

1 **to recall sth.** - *sich an etw. erinnern*
2 **to hurt sb.** - *jdm. wehtun*
3 **to brew** - *brauen*
4 **lumber yard** - *Holzlager*
5 **to leave** - *verlassen*
6 **thunder** - *Donner*

the distance. And he pushes through the snow, and he thinks that maybe, if he can get to the sound, he can **flee**[1] into the mountains and never come back.

"Look. Every year" Greg said, "hundreds of tourists come here, right? Most of them are rich, and some of them are very rich. They want to ski in the spring, **hike**[2] in the summer and spend their money in the hotel bar and the spa. Some of these people are millionaires, Brandon, millionaires. Think about that." Greg drank some more of his beer and looked around the bar. "Look at them. Their clothes are better than ours, their cars and trucks are better. Everything they have is better. And listen, I don't **hate**[3] them for that. I don't. I just know that if we ask them for a small **amount**[4], then they can pay. I mean twenty thousand. No more. If you ask for more, you have to wait, and then there is the risk that they contact the police. They can get twenty thousand from the bank at Banff. We tell them they only have six hours. We tell them to leave the money where we say or..."

"Or what, Greg? Or what?"

On that first day Brandon said no to the plan. On the second day he said no again. On the third day his truck stopped on the **highway**[5]. He had about three hundred **bucks**[6] left in the world. Sally was gone. Their **cabin**[7] by the lake was cold and empty, and there were no jobs for him anywhere.

So, on the fourth day he said yes.

The sound is louder now. Yes, it is a sound he knows. A sound he knows well. He can see nothing because of the trees, but he knows he is very near. He feels warmer now, and this

1 **to flee** - *flüchten*
2 **to hike** - *wandern*
3 **to hate** - *hassen*
4 **amount** - *Summe*
5 **highway** - *Schnellstraße*
6 **buck** *(AE, ugs.)* - *Dollar*
7 **cabin** - *Hütte*

scares him. In Canada, in the mountains, when you are cold you are okay, but when you are warm, you are in trouble.

What time is it now? He does not know. He only knows that it was three in the afternoon when they first heard the sound of the police sirens.

"We have to go!" Brandon shouted. "How? How can they know where we are?" said Greg. Brandon pulled him from the old **deserted**[1] cabin, and they ran for Greg's truck. The sound of the sirens was still in the distance, and Brandon thought that maybe they were still okay and that maybe they could leave; maybe they could escape together.

But then there was that gunshot...

And the man in the dark winter coat and black hat, who appeared from behind the trees.

So Brandon ran. And he got to the truck and **managed**[2] to drive to the road, where for a few minutes he thought he was free. But then another truck appeared on the road behind him.

"But which kid?" Brandon asked as they planned everything in Greg's cabin.

"There's a family who comes here, maybe three or four times a year. The wife is a pretty little thing with red hair. I think she has family here, or maybe she comes from the area. I don't know. The husband is rich, very rich. An American. The kid looks about eleven, and they let him walk into the town from the hotel sometimes. So we watch, and we wait. When he's alone, we take him. I phone the hotel. Six hours, that's it. That's enough time for them to get the money from Banff but not enough to do anything else like phone the cops. It's easy."

So that's what they did: they took the kid as he walked into town. There was no one on the snowy road. No one saw them,

1 **deserted** - *verlassen*
2 **to manage to do sth.** - *es schaffen, etw. zu tun*

but they covered Greg's **plates**[1] to be sure, and they **wore**[2] masks. The kid screamed at first, but they **gagged**[3] him and tied his hands. Greg made the call to the hotel, and they drove to the cabin in the Yoho national park. Then they waited. Six hours to leave them the money in a safe place. No police, or the kid dies. That is what Greg told the hotel, even if that part was not true.

So how did it all **go wrong**[4]?

There are fewer trees now, and the sound is louder, much louder. Like the shouting of a giant.

The Takakkaw **waterfalls**[5]. Brandon watches the clear water **tumble**[6] onto the rocks, through the snow and down to the frozen forest below.

Why here?

He doesn't know. He tried to escape from the truck that **chased**[7] him, but he crashed on the highway. The next thing he knew he was holding his shoulder and walking confused and weak.

The falls: so beautiful, just like when he and Greg were kids. He wants to sit down to look at them and moves closer to the edge.

But no. He cannot sit down. He is sure that the man with the gun is near.

So instead he stands on the edge. He feels warm and weak, and his shoulder hurts. And he can't remember where Greg is.

"You said it was easy," he says.

"But it wasn't," a voice **replies**[8], and Brandon turns and sees the dark coat, only this time there is no black hat: just long, red hair. And a rifle.

1 **plate** - *Nummernschild*
2 **to wear** - *tragen*
3 **to gag** - *knebeln*
4 **to go wrong** - *schiefgehen*
5 **waterfalls** - *Wasserfälle*
6 **to tumble** - *fallen*
7 **to chase** - *verfolgen*
8 **to reply** - *antworten*

"How? How did you find us? You only had a few hours to get the money."

"My husband went for the money," says the woman, rifle in one hand, black hat in the other. "But I went to the road where you took my son. I saw the **tracks**[1] from your truck, and I told the police, but I made sure I found the cabin first. I know these mountains better than they do and better than you."

"I'm sorry," Brandon says, "I really am sorry. The boy is okay. He's in the back room of the cabin."

"I know," the woman says.

"Are you going to **shoot**[2] me?" he asks.

There is only the sound of the waterfall for a moment. Then the woman turns and moves back into the trees. He feels his legs shake and falls down onto the red and white snow by the waterfall.

"*I already did*" she calls back to him as she slowly disappears from sight.

1 **track** – *Spur*
2 **to shoot sb.** – *jdn. erschießen*

→ Der **Takakkaw Wasserfall** befindet sich im Yoho Nationalpark in British Columbia. Mit seinen 254 Metern zählt er zu den höchsten Wasserfällen Kanadas. Der Wasserfall entspringt dem Daly Gletscher.

Die Region ist außergewöhnlich schön und nicht nur dank ihrer Unberührtheit ein beliebtes Ziel für Touristen und Naturliebhaber. Hier kann man Fahrradtouren machen, wandern, klettern, zelten und angeln. Im Winter kann man außerdem Skilanglaufen und Schneeschuhwandern. Im Yoho Nationalpark befindet sich zudem der Burgess-Schiefer, eine 505 Millionen Jahre alte Fossillagerstätte.

9. THE OLD SCHOOL TIE

The police car stops in the **driveway**[1] of the school, and the two detectives get out and look around. Detective Smith is older, his hair a mixture of black and grey, his **stomach**[2] large, and his expression usually unhappy. The other detective, West, is younger and thinner but with an empty look in his eye.

"Look at this place," says Smith.

In the distance the church towers, cathedral and university buildings of the city of Oxford are all **visible**[3]. Around the old but **impressive**[4] school, there are green gardens and **grounds**[5] that continue for miles, and at the windows of the building there are the thirty faces of serious young men, who watch them **strangely**[6].

"God, what kind of kid goes to a school like this?"

West nods but does not say anything. After only two weeks of working with Smith, he already knows that it is best to just nod.

"Come on," Smith says, and they walk to the entrance.

Inside, the school smells of wood and **polish**[7], and on the walls there are antique pictures of old teachers and respected students.

"Not like my school."

"**Sir**[8]?"

"I went to a **real**[9] school. A **comprehensive**[10]. You?"

1 **driveway** - *Auffahrt*
2 **stomach** - *Bauch*
3 **visible** - *sichtbar*
4 **impressive** - *imposant*
5 **grounds (pl.)** - *Anlagen*
6 **strangely** - *seltsam*
7 **polish** - *Politur*
8 **Sir?** - *Wie, bitte?*
9 **real** - *echt*
10 **comprehensive school** ≈ *Gesamtschule*

"Er, a **grammar school**[1], Sir." And Smith nods his head and says nothing.

The secretary outside the **headmaster's**[2] room tells them they can enter, but Smith stops. "Listen, West. I do the talking, you **make the notes**[3]. The best thing a good detective can do is listen and **observe**[4]. Write that down."

"Yes, Sir."

The headmaster is a man about the same age as Smith, but there the **comparison**[5] ends. Smith looks tired, old and unhappy. The headmaster, Mr Bowen, does not exactly look happy, but he looks **content**[6]. Content with his job, his life, his expensive house and his two expensive cars.

Smith hates him instantly.

The secretary, a young and pretty blonde, enters the room and sits by the table. The headmaster tells them to sit in the same voice he uses for his students.

"Miss White is here to take notes and can give you some more details about Mr Fletcher."

"Mr Fletcher?" asks Smith.

"Yes." Bowen stands by the large windows and does not look at them. "He's why you're here. Don't you know that?"

"No. The **chief inspector**[7] told us to come, but he didn't say why."

"Ah, yes, James. We play golf together. Good man. Well, the problem is that we can't find one of our members of staff: Mr Fletcher."

"A **missing person**[8]. I see. When did you last see him?"

"Miss White?

1 **grammar school** ≈ *Gymnasium*
2 **headmaster** - *Schulleiter*
3 **to make notes** - *Notizen machen*
4 **to observe** - *beobachten*
5 **comparison** - *Vergleich*
6 **content** - *zufrieden*
7 **chief inspector** - *Hauptkommissar*
8 **missing person** - *vermisste Person*

"His last class was yesterday at four. He was teaching the **upper sixth form**[1] boys. Geometry. They say he finished **class**[2] at five and left as normal."

"I see. Then he went home?"

"Mr Fletcher lives on the grounds of the school. Several of the older teachers do. He lives alone on the second floor in the east wing. Two other teachers live there, but neither saw him."

Smith is about to speak when a loud hammering sound starts, and Bowen shakes his head. "Sorry about that. **Building work**[3]. Several areas in the school are being renovated."

Smith **speaks up**[4]. "And did he leave the school last night?"

"We don't know. He normally doesn't. He takes his meals in the room. But last night he didn't call for anything."

"Is that strange?"

"Not **uncommon**[5]. Sometimes he prefers to have a sherry and a cigar and nothing more. But when he didn't come to breakfast this morning, we began to **worry**[6]."

Smith looks at the clock. "Mr Bowen, normally we need to wait forty-eight hours until we can start a missing-person investigation."

Bowen turns from the window and gives Smith an **annoyed**[7] look. "Your chief inspector said you could help. Was he wrong?"

Smith **sighs**[8] and shakes his head. "Does Mr Fletcher have any good friends here? Or more importantly, **enemies**[9]?"

"He is a **solitary**[10] man. But respected. He is the oldest teacher at Barnaby's: practically part of the building." Bowen stops and

1 **upper sixth form** ≈ *gymnasiale Oberstufe*
2 **class** - *Unterricht*
3 **building work** - *Bauarbeiten*
4 **to speak up** - *lauter sprechen*
5 **uncommon** - *ungewöhnlich*
6 **to worry** - *sich Sorgen machen*
7 **annoyed** - *verärgert*
8 **to sigh** - *seufzen*
9 **enemy** - *Feind*
10 **solitary** - *einsam*

thinks. "He doesn't like our new music teacher, Mr Cliff. Didn't they have some sort of fight recently, Miss White?"

"I don't think so," she says quietly.

"And what about the students?" Smith asks them both.

"The students?" replies Bowen in an **insulted**[1] tone. "Detective, the young men at this school are very clever and come from very important families. In a few years they will be politicians, judges or doctors. They are not criminals."

Smith breathes out with a **puff**[2]. "No. Well, I **suppose**[3] we could have a look around the school…"

"Good," says Bowen. "**Show** them **out**[4] Miss White." And the headmaster does not look at them again.

"Jesus," says Smith in the corridor. "Who does he think he is? Just because he plays golf with the chief inspector. **Waste of** bloody **time**[5] this is, West. Did you hear him? This Fletcher likes a sherry. He's drunk somewhere; that's all this is. In some pub in the city."

And West nods again.

They walk along the corridors for five minutes and reach an internal **courtyard**[6]. Outside they can see the renovation work: there is **scaffolding**[7] on the face of the old building, a new wall on the side of it, and three or four **workmen**[8] are sitting on a bench eating lunch.

They cross the courtyard, and Smith stops to pick up a **school tie**[9] on the floor by the new wall. "Politicians and doctors? They can't even dress themselves." And Smith puts the tie in his pocket.

1 **insulted** - *beleidigt*
2 **puff** - *Atemstoß*
3 **to suppose** - *vermuten*
4 **to show sb. out** - *jdn. hinausbegleiten*
5 **waste of time** - *Zeitverschwendung*
6 **courtyard** - *Innenhof*
7 **scaffolding** - *Baugerüst*
8 **workman** - *Handwerker*
9 **school tie** - *Krawatte der Schuluniform*

"Sir, look!" West says and points to the top of a tower.

"What?"

"There were two people watching us, Sir."

"And?"

"Well, just observing, Sir. Maybe there's a connection."

Smith sighs. "I do the thinking," he says. "Okay, one look, and then we go. We can also check one or two of the local pubs on the way back to the city."

The door to the tower is in another corridor, and when they open it, they hear **footsteps**[1] on the stairs. "Who's that?" Smith shouts.

The footsteps stop, and Miss White steps into view.

"You? Were you watching us from the roof?"

"No, well, not really," the secretary says quietly.

"Who else is with you…? Mr Fletcher?"

"What? No!"

"Be honest now, or there might be **trouble**[2] for you."

"It's my **fault**[3]," a voice says, and a young man steps forward. "Miss White came to speak to me."

"Oh really, and who are you?"

"I'm the music teacher, Mr Cliff."

"Ah, well. Isn't that interesting?"

"No, it's not what you think. I came here to tell Mr Cliff what the headmaster said about the argument."

"Go on."

"Look," says Cliff, "it was nothing, really. Only, Fletcher said something about Miss White: something no gentleman should say. I told him to **apologise**[4], and then we argued. But the last time I saw him was yesterday morning."

"It's true," **adds**[5] Miss White.

1 **footstep** - *Schritt*
2 **trouble** - *Ärger*
3 **fault** - *Schuld*
4 **to apologise** - *um Entschuldigung bitten*
5 **to add** - *hinzufügen*

"Well, we might need to talk to you again at another time," Smith says and turns to go back to the courtyard. But then he stops. "How did you know Mr Cliff was here, Miss White?"

The secretary **blushes**[1]. "We… meet here… sometimes… for lunch."

"Ah, I see."

Then the hammering they heard in the headmaster's office starts again, and the policemen go to the door.

"Detective," says the secretary. "You asked about the students. They hate Mr Fletcher. They say he **punishes**[2] them for every **mistake**[3]."

"Well, students normally don't like teachers, do they?"

"Fletcher is worse," says Cliff. "He's a dinosaur. I think he hits the boys sometimes, but I can't **prove**[4] it."

Smith nods. "I'm sure it's nothing."

Back in the courtyard Smith stops by the workmen, who are still sitting and eating their lunch. "Listen and observe, West. I suppose you didn't notice, but those two are having some sort of romantic affair."

"Er, well, yes I did notice, Sir."

"You did? Good. I can teach you a few things I think, West." And Smith nods to the workmen.

"Should we speak to the students, Sir?" West asks as they walk back to the car.

"What for?"

"Well, to see if they know anything."

Smith takes the tie from his pocket. "They're children, West: they can't even put a tie on. Let's get back to the city." And he throws the tie on the floor.

1 **to blush** - *erröten*
2 **to punish** - *bestrafen*
3 **mistake** - *Fehler*
4 **to prove** - *beweisen*

West nods. It's best to just nod. But there is something that does not make sense. The hammering noise. They heard it in the headmaster's office. And they heard it in the corridor with Miss White and Mr Cliff.

And he looks back at the workmen, who are enjoying a slow lunch.

But if these men are not hammering...

"Come on, West!" Smith shouts, and West nods.

Yes, it's best to just nod.

And somewhere in the dark Mr Fletcher stops hammering his foot against the new wall. He is tired now. Very tired.

He tries to remember exactly what happened. He remembers hitting that idiot of a boy Harris because he made a mistake in the geometry class. He remembers another boy telling him to stop. Then another boy. And another. And then **they were all on top of him**[1]. At first they only hit him. But then he felt school ties being **wrapped around**[2] his hands and feet and mouth. And they lifted him up and carried him to the new wall, which was nearly finished. And they put him behind it, in a deep dark corner where no one could see him and the light disappeared as they put the last **bricks**[3] in place. He tried desperately to shout, but he could not, and he tried to move, but he could not. And for a while he thought that he would die in the deep dark corner behind the wall.

But everything will be okay now, he knows. Because after hours of struggling his foot is now finally free to move.

And the police will be here soon, he is sure.

And they will hear.

So he continues to hammer his foot against the wall.

And he hopes that someone hears him soon.

1 **they were all on top of him** – *sie fielen alle über ihn her*
2 **to wrap sth. around sth.** – *etw. um etw. wickeln*
3 **brick** - *Baustein*

→ **Preparatory schools**, oder 'prep schools', sind Privatschulen, die sich darauf spezialisiert haben, die britischen Eliteschüler auf die Herausforderungen der Public Schools vorzubereiten. Die Schüler sind hier zwischen 8 und 13 Jahre alt. Im 19. Jahrhundert waren prep schools ausschließlich Internatsschulen.

Public Schools oder Independent Schools sind im Vereinigten Königreich Schulen, die durch Schulgebühren finanziert werden. Die ersten Public Schools waren damals dazu bestimmt, begabten Kindern die Chance einer Schulbildung zu vermitteln, unabhängig von der finanziellen Situation der Familie. Daher stammt die Bezeichnung Public School. Der größte Teil der Schüler waren normal zahlende Schüler.

10. THE TUBE

The air of the **tube**[1] platform is hot and dry, and the lights weak and unnatural.

Sarah considers sitting on one of the seats by the wall of the tunnel, but she is so tired that she thinks that maybe she will fall asleep if she rests.

So she stands, and she looks around at her fellow **commuters**[2] and other passengers. Twenty tired faces: some talking, but most are silent and waiting like her.

She looks at the electronic clock.

It is seven thirty-six: her train should be here in two minutes.

For a moment she thinks about how quiet the platform is, and how normally she has to **fight**[3] to get on the train in the evening.

But there will be no fighting today: the few people that are here look half dead. Exhausted from a long day at work and made passive by the slow **journey**[4] home.

Home.

Sarah thinks about her **cosy**[5] sofa and the Chinese takeaway she will eat while watching TV. She can get it as she passes the restaurant, buy a bottle of wine from the local shop and be in bed by ten o'clock.

It is a **comforting**[6] but also rather depressing thought.

But that's life.

1 **tube** - *Londoner U-Bahn*
2 **commuter** - *Pendler(in)*
3 **to fight** - *kämpfen*
4 **journey** - *Fahrt*
5 **cosy** - *gemütlich*
6 **comforting** - *beruhigend*

Work, eat, sleep.

She hears the train in the dark tunnel and tells herself to wake up and to focus for another forty minutes.

The forty minutes from Liverpool Street to North Acton.

The train **speeds**[1] out of the tunnel, and she enjoys the feeling of the wind in her dark brown hair. As it stops, she sees her reflection in the mirror of the **carriage**[2].

I look like death, she thinks.

The doors of the carriages open, a few people get off, and Sarah and the commuters get on.

Inside the carriage it is even hotter than on the platform, but it is almost empty too.

She finds a seat and sits down.

Do not **fall asleep**[3], she tells herself.

She looks around the carriage: there are only eight other people there: a young **couple**[4] holding hands and talking quietly on the seat opposite her; two businessmen a few seats to her right; an old lady two seats to her left; a mother and son at the far end of the carriage. And a strange-looking man in a coat in the corner.

A strange man.

Is he strange? Or are you just being **silly**[5]?

She looks at him. She cannot see his face because he has the **hood**[6] of his sports jacket up, but he seems to be asleep, and there is something about his face that she does not like. He has a short beard and pale, unhealthy skin, and she thinks that his eyes are probably **unkind**[7].

The train starts, and she shakes her head.

1 **to speed** - *flitzen*
2 **carriage** - *Wagen*
3 **to fall asleep** - *einschlafen*
4 **couple** - *Paar*
5 **silly** - *albern*
6 **hood** - *Kapuze*
7 **unkind** - *unfreundlich*

You are an idiot, she tells herself and pulls a book out of her bag. On the front there is a picture of a man with a short beard and pale skin and unkind eyes. She almost laughs.

You need to stop reading this **rubbish**[1]: you are **losing your mind**[2], she tells herself.

The man in the corner is probably just a normal guy and not some horrible character from one of her thrillers.

For ten minutes she reads her **crime novel**[3]. She starts to feel better: more relaxed and less **concerned**[4] about the reason why the tube is so quiet today.

Then the train stops at another station. There are loud voices on the platform and Sarah knows why.

The doors slide open, and ten or twelve students from Chancery High School enter the carriage.

The old woman two seats away from her does not look happy and she moves to sit in the seat next to Sarah.

"**Do you mind**[5], **dear**[6]?"

"No, of course not," Sarah says and smiles. The poor old woman must not feel too comfortable next to the noisy kids, but Sarah knows that they are okay: she can **spot** the bad kids **from a mile away**[7].

She is, after all, a teacher.

No, these kids are okay, but they are loud, and it is impossible for Sarah not to hear their conversation. And when she hears the **topic**[8] that they are talking about, she suddenly feels cold.

"Yeah, he killed another one, didn't he? Last Friday, they **reckon**[9]," the tallest of the kids says.

1 **rubbish** *(BE)* - *Müll*
2 **to lose one's mind** - *den Verstand verlieren*
3 **crime novel** - *Kriminalroman*
4 **concerned** - *besorgt*
5 **Do you mind?** - *Stört es Sie?*
6 **dear** - *Schatz (auch unter Fremden)*
7 **to spot sth. from a mile away** - *sofort erkennen*
8 **topic** - *Thema*
9 **to reckon** - *meinen*

"I know, sick, isn't it? I mean, how many is that now?" asks another.

"Six?"

"No, man, seven."

"Is it? Man, you know, the sick thing is that no one knows who it is. They don't know if it's a man, a woman, some kid, you **get**[1] me?"

"No, the sick thing is the way he kills them. He uses something strange: not a knife but something long and thin, and he **stabs**[2] them again and again, and they just bleed and bleed."

"Yeah, but the **weird**[3] thing is none of them tried to fight," says the tall kid.

"How do you know that?"

"**Coz**[4] the newspapers said it. They said none of the victims looked like they tried to fight. They just, I don't know, let this guy stab them again and again."

And now there is silence in the carriage, and Sarah sees that everyone is listening to the conversation.

But she does not want to listen, and she takes her MP3 player from her bag and puts her headphones in.

She does not want to think about their conversation or the horrible reason why the tube is so quiet. She does not want to think about the stories in the newspapers.

She does not want to think about what the police are calling *the tube murders.*

She closes her eyes and thinks about her sofa, her Chinese take-away and her bed. After a few more minutes she feels the train stop and she **is aware**[5] of the kids getting off.

Just listen to the music, she tells herself. Relax and rest.

1 **to get** *(BE, ugs.)* **-** *verstehen*
2 **to stab sb. -** *jdn. niederstechen*
3 **weird -** *seltsam*
4 **coz** *(ugs.)* **-** *weil*
5 **to be aware -** *merken*

But don't sleep.

Don't...

But she is **exhausted**[1], and her head begins to drop, and she feels herself falling asleep.

And she dreams about dark tunnels and strange men watching her.

Then she feels a sharp pain in her arm, and she almost screams.

She looks to see what the pain is and pulls her headphones from her ears.

"I'm sorry, dear," the old woman says, and Sarah sees that the woman's cloth bag is touching her arm. "Did I wake you up? It must be something in my bag. I have all my **knitting things**[2] in here." The old woman looks very **upset**[3] and **apologetic**[4].

"It's okay," Sarah says and smiles. "I was just surprised."

"Oh, you poor thing, you look exhausted. I'll move my bag so you can sleep."

"It's okay. I don't want to sleep."

"No, you relax," the old woman says, and Sarah thinks the old lady has a kind smile.

Sarah nods and is about to put her headphones back in her ears when she feels someone watching her, and she looks at the corner of the carriage.

The strange man, the man who looks like the evil character from her thriller; his eyes are open now.

And they are watching her.

She feels a cold shiver move over her body, and suddenly she thinks that she **feels** a little **ill**[5].

Is he watching her? She looks again and, yes, his hood is still covering his face, but she is sure that his eyes are focused on her.

1 **exhausted** - *erschöpft*
2 **knitting things** - *Strickzeug*
3 **upset** - *traurig*
4 **apologetic** - *entschuldigend*
5 **to feel ill** - *sich krank fühlen*

She tries to stay calm. There are still several people in the carriage: the young couple is still there and the two businessmen.

And the next station is North Acton, her station.

You just need to get home, she tells herself, and she feels the train **slow down**[1], and she knows she must get up.

"Is this your stop, dear?" the old woman asks.

Sarah nods.

"Oh, good. You're nearly home. Nearly time to get some sleep." Sarah tries to smile.

"Are you okay, dear? You look a little pale."

"Yes, just tired."

"You should put some water on your face. You'll feel better."

Sarah nods. "I will. Thank you."

I will, she thinks, but only if the strange man stays on the train. If he follows me, I will shout and scream for help.

She stands up and looks in the corner of the carriage one more time, but it looks like the man is asleep.

Go. Go now, she tells herself.

The doors open, and she quickly walks through them.

For a few seconds she walks and then turns back to look at the tube train. No one is there. No one gets off apart from her, she is sure.

The train starts again and she relaxes a little.

The platform at North Acton is quiet, but it always is at this time of the evening. She can see the stairs to the street, and she wants to walk to them, but she feels so weak.

She decides to go into the station toilets. All she needs is a little water.

She enters the **ladies'**[2] and stands in front of the mirror. Her arm hurts, so she takes her jacket off, and in the mirror she can see a small drop of blood on her skin.

1 **to slow down** - *bremsen*
2 **ladies'**- *Damentoilette*

"It's okay, dear, you will feel better in a moment. I gave you a little medicine to help you sleep."

Sarah jumps at the sound of the voice, and in the mirror she sees the reflection of the old woman. "What?" she tries to say, but then she falls to the floor. "Help me..." she says in a weak voice.

The old woman smiles, but it is a horrible smile. "I am helping you, dear. You poor thing. So tired, so exhausted. You can't live like that. But it's okay now: I'm here to help you."

And the old woman takes a long, thin **knitting needle**[1] from her bag, and Sarah remembers what the kid said on the tube...

... *He uses something strange: not a knife but something long and thin, and he stabs them again and again, and they just bleed and bleed.*

She tries to scream, but it is too late.

1 **knitting needle** – *Stricknadel*

The Tube, wie die Londoner ihre U-Bahn nennen, war die erste Untergrundbahn der Welt. Die Eröffnung des ersten Streckenabschnitts fand im Jahre 1863 statt. Lange hat die London Tube mit ihren 402 Kilometern den Rekord als längstes Streckennetz der Welt gehalten: Mittlerweile ist sie auf Platz drei hinter die U-Bahn-Netze von Shanghai und Peking gerutscht.

Eine Besonderheit des Londoner U-Bahn-Netzes ist, dass an den Haltestellen Personal zu finden ist, das u. a. den Fahrtgästen mit dem Kauf von Fahrtkarten an den Automaten hilft und Auskunft über den Fahrplan gibt.

Die London Tube dient aber nicht nur dem Personenverkehr: Während des Zweiten Weltkriegs wurden tief gelegene U-Bahn-Stationen als Luftschutzbunker benutzt. Außerdem trafen sich Premierminister Churchill und sein Kabinett in der heute geschlossenen Station Down Street.

11. THE ACCIDENT

It was an accident.

He was dead, but it was an accident.

Emily felt her **legs go weak**[1] and she felt like she could not breathe. The tunnels were hot, impossibly hot, and she wanted to take the **torch**[2] and run along the **passages**[3] to the entrance and then out into the **humid**[4] night of the jungle.

But she did not.

Instead she sat down, with her back against the side of the ancient Mayan **burial stone**[5] and began to cry, the noise **echoing**[6] around the small room.

Finally the tears stopped and she dried her eyes with the sleeve of her khaki shirt and pushed her brown hair away from her face.

She was not the type of person to cry for no reason, but she knew that what she had done was going to change her life forever.

Yes, it had been an accident, but even if anyone believed her, her career was over, her six years of study a **waste of time**[7].

And it was all because of him.

She **stared**[8] for a moment at his body in the dim light from the torch.

Professor Mounier.

1 **to feel one's legs go weak** - *weiche Knie bekommen*
2 **torch** - *Taschenlampe*
3 **passage** - *Gang*
4 **humid** - *schwül*
5 **burial stone** - *Grabstein*
6 **to echo** - *widerhallen*
7 **waste of time** - *Zeitverschwendung*
8 **to stare at sth.** - *etw. anstarren*

He looked extremely peaceful. He was not an ugly man, but neither was he handsome. Maybe he had been, twenty years ago, but now he was in his fifties, his stomach was large and his tanned face was covered by his beard.

No, he was not attractive. He was **repellent**[1]. A serpent, not a man. With hands that never stopped moving, touching, searching and reaching for her.

But not now. No, now he was still, his hands unmoving.

And next to his left eye there was a bloody hole where she had hit him with the small **excavation**[2] hammer.

For a moment she **felt like**[3] crying again, but she did not let herself. She had to get to the British **embassy**[4] before the body was found, explain what had happened, explain that it had not been her **fault**[5].

Not her fault.

No, it had been his.

For three months she had worked here with him in Belize, excavating a new sequence of tunnels found near to the Caana. It was every young archaeologist's dream. To work with a famous professor like Mounier, to be present at the opening of a new excavation.

But the reality had been different.

She had known that Mounier had been looking for an assistant, and she had gone to see him at his office. At the beginning everything had been **pleasant**[6]. Yes, they had been flirting a bit, but nothing more than that. But then he had become **insistent**[7] and talking about his wife was the only way to stop him.

1 **repellent** - *widerwärtig*
2 **excavation** - *Ausgrabung*
3 **to feel like doing sth.** - *Lust haben, etw. zu tun*
4 **embassy** - *Botschaft*
5 **fault** - *Schuld*
6 **pleasant** - *angenehm*
7 **insistent** - *hartnäckig*

Then tonight he had come to the tunnels where she was working alone and she had smelt the alcohol on his **breath**[1], she had seen the dangerous look in his eyes.

But it was an accident. He had tried to reach for her, and she had told him to stop, but he had not.

So she had stopped him.

She looked at the hammer. Yes, it had not been her fault.

So why should she **suffer**[2]?

And suddenly she was not thinking about the British embassy anymore. She was thinking that of all the places to hide a body, **surely**[3] these dark tunnels were the best.

She pushed herself up and looked around.

The body was behind the burial stone, but Mounier's feet could be seen if someone came.

And **someone might come**[4]. Yes, one of the other assistants, Claire or Stephen, maybe.

Quickly she reached down and grabbed him under his arms, his sweat on her hands, and she pulled him half a metre until the body was hidden.

Then for a moment she looked at the burial stone and **contemplated**[5] the possibility of placing him beneath it, but no, it was a **ridiculous**[6] idea. At some point it would be moved again, and then it would be obvious that she had placed him there.

"Think!" she told herself, but all she could do was repeat the words *it was an accident*.

An accident. Yes, that was it. The tunnels were newly excavated and still not completely **safe**[7]. She could **drag**[8] the

1 **breath** - *Atem*
2 **to suffer** - *leiden*
3 **surely** - *bestimmt*
4 **someone might come** - *jd. könnte kommen*
5 **to contemplate** - *erwägen*
6 **ridiculous** - *absurd*
7 **safe** - *ungefährlich*
8 **to drag** - *schleifen*

body down one of them and then destroy the **supports**[1] keeping the heavy stone in place. The body would be crushed and the injury from the hammer hidden.

She almost smiled. It was so simple.

Then she heard the sound of footsteps from the entrance and she **froze**[2].

"Emily?" a voice said, and then Claire was there, another torch in her hand, a smile on her face. "Are you still here?"

"Yes, nearly finished."

"I'm walking back to the camp in a moment. I can wait for you."

"Oh, no. You should go. Mounier said he wanted to inspect something."

Claire shook her head. "Yeah, right, he just wants to get you in here alone. I hate that man."

Emily saw the hammer on the floor. She tried to smile. "Look, you go, honestly. I want to speak to him too."

Claire stopped smiling, "Wait, you're not? You know? You and him?"

Emily moved in front of the murder weapon. She **vigorously**[3] shook her head. "God, no!"

Claire laughed. "Good! Okay, well. If he tries to touch you, **give him a slap**[4]. See you later."

And then Emily was alone again. She took a deep breath of the warm air and quickly picked up the hammer and put it in her pocket.

She had to be quick now.

Which was the best tunnel to leave the body in? The east passage was easier to get to, but the west passage was less

1 **support** - *Stütze*
2 **to freeze** - *erstarren*
3 **vigorously** - *energisch*
4 **to give sb. a slap** - *jdm. eine Ohrfeige geben*

secure[1]. She could easily break one or two of the supports, and the stone would **collapse**[2].

Yes, the west.

This time she took hold of Mounier by his feet and began to drag him further into the tunnel, the torch in her mouth.

For ten minutes she dragged him, and when, finally, they were at the less secure area, she stopped, sweat covering her entire body, and looked around.

It was perfect.

A few metres in front of her there were two **vertical**[3] supports and next to them was a sign that said no one should enter.

She could move the body there and then **weaken**[4] the supports.

No.

If she did that, the whole structure could collapse on top of her.

"Think!"

Then in the shadow of the tunnel she saw a **coil of rope**[5]. Yes, that was it. First she could weaken the supports, then drag the body there, and when she was ready, she could **tie**[6] the rope to a support and from a safe distance pull on it until it collapsed.

She went to the supports, leaving the body there, and began to examine them.

She had to be very careful. She had to weaken the support, but not too much.

She took the hammer from her pocket and began to destroy a little of the stone at the top of one of the supports, while constantly listening to the stone.

For ten minutes she worked, slowly and carefully, and then she moved to the other support. She thought this one already

1 **secure** - *fest*
2 **to collapse** - *einstürzen*
3 **vertical** - *senkrecht*
4 **to weaken** - *schwächen*
5 **coil of rope** - *Seilrolle*
6 **to tie** - *festbinden*

looked weaker and after just two minutes she heard the stones about her move. She froze.

Above her she could imagine the ancient pyramid and the hundreds of thousands of blocks of stone. Suddenly, she felt like she should leave the tunnels and Belize, return to Oxford and never enter this horrible place again.

But no, she could not. She had to finish this now.

She ran back to the rope and picked up one end, leaving the other by the body.

For a second, in the shadows, she thought she saw Mounier's eye move. She stopped and stared, but no, it was just a trick of the light.

He was dead. It was an accident, but he was dead.

She walked back to the support and listened.

Silence.

But that did not mean she was safe. She began to tie the rope to the support and had only just finished when she heard it.

At first she thought that it was the stone moving above her, and she believed she was in danger. But then she **realised**[1] that it was not the stone at all.

It was a weak cry of help from Mounier.

He was alive.

For a second she did not believe it, but then she saw his hands move, and his cry for help was repeated. She felt **dizzy**[2], and she had no idea what to do.

He was alive, she could still tell the embassy everything. She could tell them that he had attacked her and that it had been an accident and that she had only been trying to **defend**[3] herself.

Yes, that is what she would do.

But then she saw his hands moving; they were reaching out, searching for something to help him sit.

1 **to realise** - *sich klar werden*
2 **dizzy** - *schwindlig*
3 **to defend oneself** - *sich verteidigen*

And then his hand found the rope.

"No! Don't..." she shouted.

But it was too late. The sound of moving stone filled her ears, and **dust**[1] filled her mouth and eyes. Then everything went black.

Mounier never remembered how he had got so far into the tunnel or exactly what had happened to his assistant. But he knew what to say to the police and the reporters – and to her parents.

And no one could disagree.

Because it had been, obviously, exactly how he described it.

An accident.

1 **dust** – *Staub*

→ **Belize** ist das einzige Land Zentralamerikas, in dem Englisch die offizielle Amtssprache ist. Heutzutage ist bekannt, dass Belize mitten im Herzen des Gebietes liegt, das die Maya ehemals bewohnt haben. In Belize sind über 900 archäologische Fundstätten zu finden, wo einige der ältesten archäologischen Funde ausgegraben wurden, wie z.B. die Ruine „Cuello" in der Nähe von Orange Walk Town. Viele dieser beeindruckenden Fundstätten befinden sich in sehr abgelegenen Dschungelgegenden. Andere, wie Altun Ha und Xunantunich, liegen sehr nahe an Hauptverkehrsstraßen.

12. COLD HEART

"They say the weather is going to change." John said, looking out of the window of the car as it moved slowly along the quiet road.

Next to him his wife, Jill, continued to drive in silence, and he knew she was still not happy.

For a while he said nothing and enjoyed looking at the snow-covered Lancashire countryside. They had left Manchester half an hour ago and the grey of the city had slowly changed to white.

"It's nearly March. They say this snow should be gone in a few days."

That horrible silence again.

"Jill?"

She turned to look at him for a second, and he thought that his wife could sometimes look extremely **terrifying**[1].

"Jill, I only said that maybe he's gone because she's always..."

"Always what?" Jill **snapped**[2], and John knew this was a dangerous conversation.

"You know. Hard. She can be very hard."

Jill shook her head. "She's my best friend, John."

"Well, he's my best **mate**[3]," John said **defensively**[4], "and the things he used to say about her..."

"What?"

"Well, she never let him go to the pub. She didn't like him playing football with us on Sunday mornings."

1 **terrifying** - *furchterregend*
2 **to snap** - *aufschnappen*
3 **mate** - *Kumpel*
4 **defensively** - *verteidigend*

"And you think that is a good reason to leave your wife and two children, do you?"

A very dangerous conversation.

They drove in silence for the next five miles until they reached Rawtenstall, a quiet Lancashire town of grey **terraced houses**[1] and forgotten **cotton mills**[2].

Jill parked the car and then turned to her husband.

"I'm going to ask you one more time. Do you know where he is?"

John shook his head. "I've told you a hundred times. No."

Jill looked at him carefully. "And he hasn't phoned you? Sent you any **texts**[3]?"

"No, I promise."

Jill was dangerously silent for another moment. "And tell me the truth, is there another woman?"

The truth. What could he say to that? It was true that he had not seen Phil, that he had not received any calls from him. However, he could not tell her the truth about Phil **in regards to**[4] other women.

How could he? What could he say?

That he was **cheating**[5] **on** his wife? That he had at least three or four women that he was constantly **texting**[6] or calling from his secret **mobile**[7]?

No. Obviously he could not say that.

"I don't know. He's never said anything to me about another woman."

For another moment Jill said nothing, but then she shook her head. "Okay, but if he calls or texts you, I want to know."

1 **terraced house** - *Reihenhaus*
2 **cotton mill** - *Baumwollspinnerei*
3 **text (message)** - *SMS*
4 **in regards to** - *bezüglich*
5 **to cheat on sb.** - *jdn. betrügen*
6 **to text** - *simsen*
7 **mobile (phone)** - *Handy*

"Yes, dear," John said, and they got out of the car.

Was Phil with one of his other women?

At first John had thought that he was, but after two weeks he had begun to worry. He had tried to call Phil's secret mobile, the one that Sally did not know about, but there was no reply. And his office knew nothing either: he had not been to work once, and he had not emailed or called them.

"Do you think maybe he's had an accident?" John asked as they walked through the snow towards the house.

"I hope he has because no other reason is good enough. Poor Sally. And those beautiful kids of theirs. If he hasn't had an accident, I will kill him if I ever see him again."

John **shivered**[1], but he was not sure if it was because of the cold or because of the tone of his wife's voice.

They reached the door of the house.

"Do we have to stay for long?"

Jill gave him a hard look and pressed the **doorbell**[2].

"I hope she's okay, the poor..."

Then the door opened, and Sally was there. John had always found Sally extremely beautiful, with her warm smile, her friendly eyes and those eyebrows which accompanied every word she said. At least normally.

However, she did not look like this today.

No, today Sally looked completely different. Her hair was **untidy**[3] and unwashed. Her eyes were **dull**[4] and tired and had large purple circles under them. And her face looked like it could not smile and that it never had smiled.

"Sally," said Jill. "Oh, Sally, how are you?"

For a moment Sally did not seem to hear and continued to look at them with a strange expression on her face.

1 **to shiver** - *erschaudern*
2 **doorbell** - *Türklingel*
3 **untidy** - *zerstrubbelt*
4 **dull** - *stumpf*

"Oh, Jill, John. You're here."

"Yes, we said we were coming today. Don't you remember?"

Sally nodded. "Of course, of course. Come in," she said and walked back into the house.

For a moment they **hesitated**[1]. "Jesus, she looks..." John began.

"Shh, come on."

They had been to Sally and Phil's place hundreds of times, but the house had never looked like this. Normally the small but attractive terraced house was perfectly organised and **immaculately**[2] clean. However, today there were children's toys lying on every inch of the floor, baskets of dirty clothes blocking the hallway and a smell of rubbish and old food from the kitchen.

They found Sally in the **lounge**[3] sitting on the sofa and watched as she poured herself a glass of wine.

"Drink?" she said, but John and Jill both shook their heads.

"Oh, Sally, you **poor thing**[4]. Do you still know nothing?"

Sally looked confused for a moment, and then unexpectedly she laughed. "No, Jill, I know everything. Everything."

"What? You know where Phil is?"

She laughed again. "Oh yes. But I know a lot more than that. I know about the other women. I found his phone. I read all his dirty messages."

"Other women?" Jill said, and she gave John a quick, terrifying look.

"Lots. I don't know how many."

"Oh my God. How could he? The monster. I always thought he had a cold heart, but I never thought..."

"What?" Sally said, a strange expression growing on her face. "What did you say?"

1 **to hesitate** - *zögern*
2 **immaculately** - *makellos*
3 **lounge** - *Salon*
4 **poor thing** - *armes Ding*

"I... just that Phil has a cold heart."

And for a moment it seemed like Sally might cry, but she began to laugh instead and she laughed so hard that her hand shook and the wine splashed from the glass onto the coffee table.

Jill looked at John in **confusion**[1], but he shook his head.

"What, Sally? What is it?" Jill asked, and she went to sit next to her friend and took the glass of wine from her.

"A cold heart! Ha, oh yes, oh yes! That's good, that's very good!" Sally said, and she laughed for another minute before she finally stopped.

"But do you know where he is now?" Jill asked.

"Oh, yes, of course."

"You do? Where?"

"He's here."

"Here?" John asked, surprised.

"Won't you have a drink?" Sally said to Jill.

"But where is he?" John asked again.

"Oh, he's outside in the garden, with the kids."

"But the other women?" Jill asked.

"Oh, there won't be any more of them," Sally said, and she smiled in a way that made John feel cold.

"I think I'll go say hello," he said, but the two women ignored him.

He walked to the kitchen, which was dirty, the bin full and rubbish in bags next to it, and he looked out of the window. The garden was white, the snow half a metre high, and he could see the kids, little Sammy and Sarah, playing in the snow.

But he could not see Phil.

He went to the door and opened it. "Hey, kids," he shouted, and they waved at him and smiled.

"Where's your dad then?" But their faces were **blank**[2], and they shook their heads.

1 **confusion** - *Verwirrung*
2 **blank** - *ausdruckslos*

"He must be upstairs, hey?" he said, and he shut the door, and they began to play again. Making snowballs and throwing them at the large snowman in the middle of the garden.

"I made a mistake," Sally said behind him, and John jumped with **fright**[1]. He turned round and looked at her.

"Where's Phil?"

"I was confused," Sally said, her voice strange. "I have not been sleeping very well. Phil's not here. I don't know where he is."

John nodded. "I see."

And for the next two hours Jill helped to tidy the house and talked to Sally and told her that Phil was a monster. Then it was time to go.

"Goodbye then," Jill said. "I'll come back in a few days, but if you need anything, you call me, okay?"

Sally nodded and **showed them to the door**[2], and John felt like he should say something, but he did not know what.

"Oh well, everything will be okay, hey? And at least the weather is improving. All this snow should be gone in a few days."

"What?" Sally said, and she grabbed his arm, "What did you say?"

And her fingers pressed into his skin so hard that he almost shouted for her to stop.

"The weather… is improving," he said.

"The snow… you said… the snow…."

And then something horrible occurred to John. No, it could not possibly be true.

"Sally? Phil… you didn't?"

Sally smiled. Then she began to laugh again, and in between the laughter she repeated two words.

Two words.

John took his phone from his pocket and pushed past Sally. He went into the kitchen and opened the back door.

1 **fright** - *Erschrecken*
2 **to show sb. to the door** - *jdn. zur Tür bringen*

"What are you doing, John?" Jill shouted.
Two words.
He pressed "call" on the number of Phil's secret phone and walked out into the snow and stood before the snowman.
It was true: from somewhere deep inside the snow, he heard the sound of a ringing phone.
Behind him he heard Sally laughing and Jill shouting.
But he could only think about those two words.
"Cold heart."

→ Die Stadt Rawtenstall liegt in der Grafschaft **Lancashire** im Nordwesten Englands, der als die Wiege der industriellen Revolution gilt. Die Gegend ist berühmt für ihre Rolle in der Geschichte der Industrie im ausgehenden 18. Jahrhundert und die daraus resultierende Architektur. Zunächst herrschte die Baumwollindustrie vor, die auch eine sehr rasante Entwicklung erfuhr. Diese Entwicklung bescherte der Region ein hochentwickeltes Transportsystem zu Land und Wasser. Beispielhaft dafür ist die weltweit erste Städteverbindung mit der Eisenbahn zwischen Manchester und Liverpool.

13. THE LOCKED ROOM

Victoria looked out of the glass **elevator**[1] and watched the city of Houston in front of her.

The city was a sea of lights and the lift continued to **rise**[2] until she was higher than all of the other **skyscrapers**[3].

She turned to the handsome Japanese man who stood silently next to her and **shook her head**[4]. "I still don't understand what I'm doing here," she said as they continued to rise.

Mr Ichiro nodded. "I know, and I'm sorry to wake you at this time of the night, but when you agreed to write for the Teikoku Company, you signed a contract… And in this contract you agreed to be **available**[5] for Mr Kenta at any time."

"You always say that, but I don't remember any **agreement**[6]. And what type of assistance can he need from me? I'm a writer, a **novelist**[7]."

Ichiro nodded. "I know. You met Mr Kenta when you started to work at the company; he was very pleased to meet you."

"He's a nice man, and he seems to like my writing, but I still don't understand why he needs to see me."

"Ah, no, he doesn't. You don't understand. You can't see Mr Kenta, but he wants you to help me with a problem. He was always very impressed with your stories and your beautifully complex plots[8]."

1 **elevator** *(AE)* - *Aufzug*
2 **to rise** - *hinaufsteigen*
3 **skyscraper** - *Wolkenkratzer*
4 **to shake one's head** - *den Kopf schütteln*
5 **available** - *verfügbar*
6 **agreement** - *Vereinbarung*
7 **novelist** - *Schriftsteller(in)*
8 **plot** - *Handlung*

Victoria looked at Ichiro: the man's English was almost perfect, but for a moment she thought he had made a mistake. "You said, he *was* always impressed."

And then she saw the emotion that Ichiro was trying to **hide**[1]. "Yes, Mr Kenta is dead. He was killed this evening. Murdered."

It took Victoria a moment to understand. "He's dead? But you said that he wanted me to help you."

"That's correct. Mr Kenta left a very detailed **will**[2]. In his will he stated that if he died **in mysterious circumstances**[3], he wanted you to assist me in identifying his killer."

"What? That's crazy. You don't need me, you need the police."

"The police are here, but the Teikoku Company is very powerful, and the Houston police have agreed to you seeing the **murder scene**[4]." The lift stopped, and Ichiro looked at her.

The metal doors opened and outside two **paramedics**[5] and a Houston cop were waiting. Between them a **gurney**[6], which was carrying a black **body bag**[7].

Mr Ichiro **bowed**[8] and looked at the bag with an expression of sadness. "Please wait in the car park for me. I wish to travel to the hospital with the body."

The cop nodded, and Victoria stepped from the lift so they could enter.

Ichiro passed her a pair of latex gloves. "I know you are familiar with crime scenes because of your research, but remember to touch nothing without these."

1 **to hide** - *verbergen*
2 **will** - *Testament*
3 **in mysterious circumstances** - *unter mysteriösen Umständen*
4 **murder scene** - *Tatort*
5 **paramedic** - *Sanitäter(in)*
6 **gurney** (*AE*) - *Rollbahre*
7 **body bag** - *Leichensack*
8 **to bow** - *sich verbeugen*

Victoria watched the elevator door close. "Okay, but if this is real, if you want my help, **shouldn't I**[1] see the body?"

"You can, if you wish, but I examined it," Ichiro said, "and I can tell you he was killed by a knife or **dagger**[2] to his heart. It looks professional. He died... without pain."

Victoria nodded.

"That, however, is not the problem. The problem is how the murderer escaped. Follow me."

They walked along a luxurious **corridor**[3] to a large golden door where two policemen and two private security guards were waiting.

Ichiro nodded and a security guard opened the door.

The room inside was more spectacular than any other room Victoria had ever seen. It was like a Japanese palace in the sky, with **elaborate**[4] decorations, modern and classical art, expensive furniture and every type of electronic device possible.

"Yes, when you met Mr Kenta, you saw his private offices. This is his personal apartment within the Teikoku Company. It was his place to connect to his origins in Japan. Mr Kenta needed this."

There were blood stains on the white carpets and the black leather sofas. "Did he die here?"

"Yes."

"Did you find him?"

"I did. I'm Mr Kenta's head of security," he said, and Victoria could hear the **shame**[5] in his voice.

"I saw cameras in the corridor."

1 **shouldn't I...** - *sollte ich nicht...*
2 **dagger** - *Dolch*
3 **corridor** - *Flur*
4 **elaborate** - *kunstvoll*
5 **shame** - *Schamgefühl*

"Yes, but there are **none**[1] in here. He was a **private man**[2]. And I assured him that he was **safe**[3] here... but I was wrong."

"Why did you think he was safe?"

"Because there is only one **access point**[4] to this room: the corridor. The only other way is to **climb**[5] the glass walls of the building and enter one of the windows here. That climb is almost impossible, and the windows can only be opened from inside. But more than this, the apartment is protected by one of the best security systems in the world, imported from Japan, and **nobody but**[6] Mr Kenta and I knew the activation words. Watch." Ichiro said something in Japanese.

Suddenly there was movement in every part of the room, and metal screens fell from the roof on the inside and outside of the windows. The golden door closed **instantly**[7], and Victoria heard an electronic lock connect.

"**As soon as that command is given**[8] the police are informed, I am informed, my team is informed."

"Impressive, but obviously Mr Kenta didn't have enough time to give the command."

Ichiro shook his head. "You don't understand. When I arrived the room was locked."

Victoria thought for a second and then she suddenly understood. "Then the killer didn't escape. If Kenta died instantly, he probably gave the command a second before his death."

"Exactly," said Ichiro, and Victoria noticed for the first time that his hand was always near to the gun under his jacket.

"You think he's still in this room?"

1 **none** - *keine*
2 **private man** - *zurückhaltender Mann*
3 **safe** - *in Sicherheit*
4 **access point** - *Zugangspunkt*
5 **to climb** - *klettern*
6 **nobody but** - *niemand außer*
7 **instantly** - *augenblicklich*
8 **As soon as that command is given...** - *Sobald dieser Befehl erteilt wird...*

"It's impossible. We've **searched**[1] every place a man could hide. The police and my team tell me that there is nobody here."

"What do you think?"

"I think this system is the best. When Mr Kenta gave the command, the room was locked. How could the killer escape?"

Victoria nodded. It was, indeed, like the **plot** of one of her **novels**[2]: an impossible murder.

She walked around the room slowly and for some time considered the possibilities. They were few.

Could the killer still be here?

"Did your men check the outside of the building? Perhaps there was a delay in the system."

"They are checking now. A helicopter searched the glass walls but saw nobody. The men are searching some of the lower levels."

Victoria was silent. She watched Ichiro. "There is another possibility," she began.

"Yes, there is."

"You're the only other person who can control the security system. You were the first to find the body."

Ichiro looked at her. "Mr Kenta was correct: you are good. But I can assure you that I was in the security room. I have **witnesses**[3] and there is video evidence. But more than this, I can tell you that Mr Kenta was like a father to me. He brought me from Japan to Houston. I will find his killer and I will find the people who paid the killer, **for**[4] I believe this was an **assassination**[5] by a rival American company. They were jealous of our success. I am guilty only of my **inability**[6] to protect him."

Victoria said nothing, but she believed the man.

1 **to search** - *durchsuchen*
2 **novel** - *Roman*
3 **witness** - *Zeuge/Zeugin*
4 **for** - *denn*
5 **assassination** - *Ermordung*
6 **inability** - *Unfähigkeit*

She **was about to**[1] speak, when Ichiro's radio broke the silence. For a moment the head of security listened and Victoria saw a dark expression on his face.

"What? What is it?" she asked.

"They have found a body. Thirteen floors below on the roof of the second tower. I think I woke you for no reason, but thank you."

Victoria nodded, but she did not move.

"What is it?" asked Ichiro, seeing her doubt.

"It makes no sense. How could the killer escape? Mr Kenta gave the command the second before his death, and the room locked. There was no time for the killer to go back to the window."

Ichiro nodded. "Perhaps there was a **fault in the system**[2]?"

"And now there is no fault? **I don't think so**[3]." And she moved to the window again and looked at the city of Houston and the sea of lights and watched an ambulance racing through the streets.

And suddenly she understood: "Ichiro, the body: can they identify it?"

"No: the fall was too high. It's impossible to recognise."

"And after the murder was there always someone here in the room?"

"No, but there were always guards at the door, and the helicopter was also there."

"No one climbed down, Ichiro: they fell. I'm sorry, but the body they have found is Mr Kenta."

"What?"

"I think that for a few moments after the paramedics arrived, after they placed Mr Kenta's body in the bag, the room was empty, but the killer was still here."

"We searched the room."

1 **to be about to do sth.** - *im Begriff sein, etw. zu tun*
2 **fault in the system** - *Systemfehler*
3 **I don't think so.** - *Ich glaube nicht.*

"Yes, but before or after the paramedics arrived?"

"Before and after."

"But there are many places to hide, and I think that when you first looked, you didn't find him, but he was here. Then, later, after the paramedics arrived, you looked in every possible place, but he was gone."

"How? He didn't walk out the door."

"No, he didn't: he was pushed… on a gurney."

And for a second Ichiro did not understand, but then his expression changed, and he ran through the golden door to the lift, his hand on his gun.

But Victoria knew that it was too late: **he would find**[1] only two dead paramedics, a dead cop and an empty body bag.

1 **he would find...** - *er würde finden...*

Houston wurde 1836 von zwei Unternehmern aus New York gegründet. Die Stadt hatte im Jahr 1900 noch weniger als 50.000 Einwohner. Doch kurz danach wurde der Hafen eröffnet und die Stadt begann unaufhaltsam zu wachsen. Heute ist sie mit 2,2 Millionen Einwohnern die viertgrößte Stadt in den USA und der Hafen gilt als der wichtigste Hafen Amerikas. Wegen des Mission Control Centers, das sich hier befindet, trägt Houston den Spitznamen Space City. Von hier aus hat die NASA viele Fahrten ins All begleitet, unter anderem den berühmten Apollo 11 Flug. Übrigens lautete die berühmte Meldung der Astronauten damals nicht „Houston, we have a problem", wie häufig wiedergegeben wird, sondern Jack Swigert meldete an die Bodenstation: „Okay, Houston, we've had a problem here."

14. THE HONEY TRAP

Charles loved New York in the summer time. It was an absolute paradise for a man of his profession, and this evening he was feeling extremely happy about his recent work.

He **sat back**[1] in his chair at the small coffee shop table and watched the hundreds of people **stroll**[2] past him. Occasionally, he saw something that made him laugh, things that maybe you or I would not find funny, such as a **visible**[3] wallet in the back pocket of a man's jeans, or an open bag on the shoulder of a woman.

To you or me these things would not be **amusing**[4]: **in fact**[5], we would not even notice them. To Charles, however, they were a constant source of pleasure.

Charles was a perfectly normal man. There was absolutely nothing unusual about his appearance. He was of average height and weight, with ordinary brown hair and an **unremarkable**[6] face.

He was the type of man that nobody ever remembered.

And this is what made Charles very good at his job.

He saw the waitress and politely **signaled**[7] **to** her. "The bill, please."

"**Oh my gosh!**[8] Are you English? What an **awesome**[9] accent you have."

1 **to sit back** - *sich zurücklehnen*
2 **to stroll** - *schlendern*
3 **visible** - *sichtbar*
4 **amusing** - *amüsierend*
5 **in fact** - *eigentlich*
6 **unremarkable** - *unscheinbar*
7 **to signal to sb.** - *jdm. ein Zeichen geben*
8 **Oh my gosh!** - *Oh mein Gott!*
9 **awesome** *(AE, ugs.)* - *super*

She placed the bill for his drink on the table.

Charles smiled and put down five dollars. "Thank you very much. Please, keep the change."

"Thank you!" she smiled and began to walk away.

"Oh, excuse me? **I don't suppose you can change a twenty**[1]? I need some dollar **bills**[2] for the **subway**[3]."

"**Sure!**[4] Here you go, ten ones and a ten."

"Excellent," Charles said, taking the notes. "Oh, look, actually I have some **change**[5] here. Now I think I have too much. Could I change the ones back for a ten?"

"Of course," said the waitress with another smile. "Here's your ten."

He took it and seemed to put it in his wallet. "And here are your dollars," he said with an apologetic smile. "Is that right?"

"I'm sure it is… oh no, that's only nine dollars," she said and put the dollars on the table for him to see.

"Oh dear, this American money, it all looks the same to me. Well, because I have change I can take my twenty back. There's nine there, so I can give you a one and a ten, right?"

The waitress smiled again but looked a little confused now. "Oh, of course, and here's your twenty."

"Excellent. Thank you," he said, and the waitress watched him walk away.

Charles shook his head and looked at the ten dollars that he had just made, but he did not **feel** any **sympathy for**[6] the poor waitress. His motto was that if a person could be **conned**[7], they should be conned.

1 **I don't suppose you can change a twenty?** – *Könnten Sie einen Zwanziger wechseln?*
2 **bill** *(AE)* – *Geldschein*
3 **subway** *(AE)* – *U-Bahn*
4 **Sure!** *(ugs.)* – *Klar!*
5 **change** – *Kleingeld*
6 **to feel sympathy for sb.** – *mit jdm. Mitleid haben*
7 **to con sb.** *(ugs.)* – *jdn. betrügen*

A little further along the road, he saw another cafe, and outside two women were sitting and talking. One of their **purses**[1] was on their table.

He smiled and took his map of New York from his pocket.

"**G'day!**[2] I don't suppose you can help me?" he said in a strong Australian accent.

The two women looked at him with interest. "Sure, what's the problem?"

"I'm looking for this street," he said and put the map over the table, so they could see.

"Oh, that's easy, just turn left here."

"Really? Well, that's great ladies, thanks a lot."

And they watched him go with smiles on their faces too, and neither noticed that the purse was no longer on the table.

Charles was happy as he entered the park, but these small tricks were only **for his amusement**[3]. **Shortly**[4] he would meet his assistant, and the real work could start.

He approached the bench where they had arranged to meet, but she was not there. He looked at his watch; there were still a few minutes left.

Nearby[5] a violinist was playing music and seven or eight people had stopped to listen. One man had his jacket over his shoulder and Charles could see his wallet.

Not easy, he thought, but not impossible.

The violinist's song finished, and Charles stepped forward to place some money in the case at the musician's feet. **Nobody seemed to notice that**[6] instead of giving a dollar he took three.

Then he turned, took his newspaper from under his arm and started to open it. Unfortunately, it seemed that he had not

1 **purse** - *Geldbeutel*
2 **G'day! (*AUS*)** - *Guten Tag!*
3 **for his amusement** - *zu seinem Vergnügen*
4 **shortly** - *in Kürze*
5 **nearby** - *in der Nähe*
6 **Nobody seemed to notice that...** - *Niemand schien zu bemerken, dass...*

seen the man with the jacket over his shoulder. He apologised for accidentally **bumping into**[1] him. He then continued to walk with the man's wallet safely hidden in his newspaper.

He sat on the bench and hid his new items in the many pockets in his brown suit. And then he saw her.

His new assistant, Honey.

"Hey, Charles," she said.

"Good evening, Honey. You're late."

"Relax, he won't be here for another five minutes."

"Yes, but we need to make sure you understand the plan."

"Of course I do: it's exactly the same as with the other guys," she said in her strong New York accent.

Charles nodded. She was right. The plan was the same, but she did not seem to realise that this time it was for real. The other two guys they had **trapped**[2] were just for practice. Sure, they had made a little money, but tonight they could make a lot.

"And are you sure he's going to kiss you out here? I mean, he needs to be careful."

"Oh, I'm sure. I told him I don't want to meet him in some horrible hotel room. That if he likes me he can meet me outside. So I guess he might do something with his hair or wear a hat, you know, like a **disguise**[3]."

"True. But if he does, you have to make sure that when you kiss him I can see his face."

"No problem."

"Are you sure you saw his account properly? Are you sure he can withdraw five **grand**[4]?"

"I watched him do it the other day. He has a five grand limit. I mean, the guy is rich, really rich."

1 **to bump into sb.** - *mit jdm. zusammenstoßen*
2 **to trap sb.** - *jdn. in die Falle locken*
3 **disguise** - *Tarnung*
4 **grand** *(ugs., pl.)* - *(Geldscheine) Riesen, Tausender*

"Okay, so after we trap him, I take him to the **ATM**[1] and then we meet back here. Remember: if anything goes wrong, you don't know me."

"Sure, I don't know you."

"I'm serious, Honey. If the police find out that we're working together, we're in trouble."

"Okay."

Charles nodded, looked at her golden dress and beautiful hair and almost felt sorry for the guy.

Then he moved into the trees near the bench and took the camera from around his neck.

For a few minutes he watched his assistant sitting alone on the bench. Then he noticed a well-dressed good-looking man walking in her direction. The man was wearing sunglasses and kept his face down to the ground. He sat down next to Honey and they began to talk. Then, after a while, the man took her hand and moved closer to her. Charles saw Honey remove his sunglasses.

Yes, it was him, Mr Harris, the **CEO**[2] of Harris Enterprises.

Honey smiled and put her arm around him. For a second Harris did nothing, but he could not **resist her charms**[3] for long, and soon he kissed her.

Charles took the photo, and then came out from his hiding position.

"**What the hell**[4]? What are you doing?" Harris shouted.

"Sorry Mr Harris, but she paid me to," he said in a perfect Scottish accent.

Harris looked at Honey. "Honey?"

"No, not her, Mrs Harris, your wife."

"What? No!"

1 **ATM** *(AE)* - *Geldautomat*
2 **CEO (Chief Executive Officer)** - *Geschäftsführer(in)*
3 **to resist sb.'s charms** - *dem Charme von jdm. widerstehen*
4 **What the hell?** *(ugs.)* - *Was zum Teufel?*

"**Aye**[1], I'm a private detective. She contracted me to follow you and to take photos of... well, this type of activity."

Harris' face went white. "God, no, I'm ruined. She's gonna tell the press. My business, my clients. I'm gonna lose everything."

"You creep. You never told me you were married!" Honey shouted, and she stood up, her face furious, and walked in the direction of the park's exit.

"Sorry, **pal**[2], but it's my job."

"Look, you said she paid you," said Harris. "How much?"

Charles hesitated.

"Whatever it is, I can give you double."

"Double? Well, Mrs Harris said she would give me three grand for a photo."

"Three grand? Right, then I'll give you six."

"I don't know. Can you get it now?"

Harris hesitated. "Well, I can get you five now."

"You said six."

Harris nodded. "Okay, I have about a grand in my wallet, but I need to go to the ATM for the other five."

"Yeah, well I think I'll come with you," Charles said, trying not to smile.

But when they got to the ATM, Harris began to search his wallet.

"Jesus!" he shouted. "My card, I don't have my card!"

"What?"

"Look, take the grand for now, and let me send you the rest."

Charles agreed. He had to, but he was sure he would never see the money. All Harris had to do was say something to his wife, and he would realise it was all a con.

Alone and unhappy, Charles walked back to the park to find Honey.

1 **aye** *(Schottisch)* **-** *ja*
2 **pal -** *Kumpel*

A perfect evening ruined because the idiot had lost his card.

Lost his card?

He remembered the way Honey had put her arm around him. He remembered how Honey had said she had seen his account.

Did she know his **PIN**[1] too?

A **suspicion**[2] began to form in Charles' mind.

In that moment he saw Honey, a hundred metres in front of him, near to the bench.

And he saw the cop that was holding her by the arm.

Then Honey saw him, and Charles saw her point in his direction, and the cop looked too.

And that is when Charles decided to run.

"Is that him, miss? Why's he running?" the cop asked Honey.

"Yeah, that's the man who helped me when I fell over. Thank you, my leg feels better now," she said, in a perfect English accent. "But I don't know why he's running: he seemed like such a nice man," she added.

She thought about the five thousand dollars she had just withdrawn from the ATM and she smiled. But she almost felt sorry to lose such a good assistant as Charles.

1 **PIN** - *Geheimzahl*
2 **suspicion** - *Verdacht*

Der **Central Park**, auch grüne Lunge New Yorks genannt, fehlt in keinem Reiseführer über die Stadt. Es lohnt sich, ihn von einem der Wolkenkratzer aus der unmittelbaren Umgebung einmal von oben zu betrachten, um die Größe seiner Anlage zu begreifen. Diese macht mit über 349 Hektaren etwa 4 Prozent der Bodenfläche Manhattans aus. Die Bauarbeiten für den Park begannen 1858 und ließen auf dem ehemaligen Sumpfgelände einen See, ein ganzes Netz an Straßen und Pfaden, einen Zoo, eine Burg und vieles mehr entstehen. Die Planer des Parks galten 1859-60 als größter Arbeitgeber der Stadt und konnten es sich erlauben, die Bauarbeiter unter unwürdigen Bedingungen arbeiten zu lassen, da „problematische" Arbeitskräfte leicht ersetzt werden konnten.

15. THE MURDER MYSTERY

Detective Harp lifted an old newspaper above his head and ran from his car to the entrance of Heartfelt **Manor**[1]. The night was dark and wet, the storm was still over the mountains of the Lake District, and by the time he had reached the door his dark hair and beard were **dripping**[2] with rain water.

In the hallway Sergeant Sloane was waiting for him, the officer's face as white as a ghost.

"Where is everyone, Sloane?"

"It's just me here, sir. There was an accident on the old road, and no other officers can get here at the moment. But I'm glad you're here, sir: this is a real mess."

Harp nodded and looked around. He had lived near to Heartfelt Manor for twenty years, but he had never been inside. It was even more luxurious than he had imagined, with expensive portraits and the heads of **stags**[3] and other animals on the walls, and a blood-red carpet that covered the large **staircase**[4].

"So what do you know, Sloane?"

"Not much, sir. The **body**[5] is in the library. There are seven people in the house: Mr and Mrs Grey, their three guests and two employees, the cook and the **maid**[6]. At approximately half past eight there was a **power cut**[7], probably because of the

1 **manor (house)** - *Herrenhaus*
2 **to drip** - *tropfen*
3 **stag** - *Hirsch*
4 **staircase** - *Treppenhaus*
5 **body** - *Leiche*
6 **maid** - *Dienstmädchen*
7 **power cut** - *Stromausfall*

storm, and everyone heard a scream. The maid was the first to find the body. I've asked her and the cook to stay in the kitchen for now, and the others are in the **conservatory**[1]."

"Show me the body," Harp said, and he followed Sloane to the library.

The room was large and cold, and the fire in the corner looked like it had been **extinguished**[2] earlier that evening. There were only a few weak electric lights to **illuminate**[3] the scene and the hundreds of books that **lined**[4] the walls.

The body was at the table, a strange knife sticking out from his back, and a pool of blood around him on the floor.

"It's like something from that game, isn't it, sir? You know, the library, the conservatory, a dead body. And we have to find out who did it."

Harp shook his head. "This is not a game: this is a real murder," he said, but Harp knew what Sloane meant, and he remembered that he had always hated that game when he was a child.

"Yes, sir. Sorry sir," Sloane said.

"It's alright," Harp said with half a smile. "Maybe the butler did it, hey?"

"No, sir," said Sloane, not noticing the joke, "this is the butler, sir."

Harp looked at the black suit the man was wearing and saw that Sloane was right.

"What do we do, sir?"

Harp looked around the room more carefully. There was a collection of **letter openers**[5] next to some writing equipment on the desk, and Harp believed this is where the murder weapon had come from. By the extinguished fire there was a half-empty

1 **conservatory** - *Wintergarten*
2 **to extinguish** sth. - *etw. (aus)löschen*
3 **to illuminate** - *beleuchten*
4 **to line** - *säumen*
5 **letter opener** - *Brieföffner*

jug[1] of water next to two unused glasses. He walked to the fire and looked at it carefully. On top of it were the **remains**[2] of some sort of papers, destroyed by the flames and water so that they were now impossible to read.

"Alibi and motive," he said. "I want to speak to Mr Grey and his guests. I will speak to them all at the same time, and we can see if their stories **match**[3]."

"And the cook and the maid?"

"No, not until later."

And Harp followed Sloane back into the hallway.

"Is it true then?" said a woman's voice, and they turned to see a **middle-aged**[4] woman in a white uniform, "Is he dead? Is Edmund really dead?"

"I'm sorry, but yes."

The woman nodded, and Harp could see tears in her eyes.

"He was not exactly a good man, you know, but he was okay with me. Here," and the cook passed Harp a large file of papers. "Edmund told me that if anything ever happened to him I must give this to the police."

"What is it?"

"I don't know. He just said it was important."

Harp nodded but did not open the file: he had no time for this now as he needed to speak to the guests.

"Sloane, take her back to the kitchen and take statements from her and the maid. Is this the conservatory?" he asked, looking at two large glass doors.

Sloane nodded, and Harp pushed open the doors.

Inside the conservatory five faces turned to look at him, and Harp had the very clear **sensation**[5] that one of these people was his murderer.

1 **jug** - *Krug*
2 **remain** - *Rest*
3 **to match** - *übereinstimmen*
4 **middle-aged** - *mittleren Alters*
5 **sensation** - *Gefühl*

"My name is Detective Harp. I need to speak to you about what happened this evening."

A tall man with white hair stepped forwards. "I'm Mr Grey; this is my wife Jennifer," he said, looking at a much younger and very attractive blonde. "These are our guests, Alexander Pine, Miss Olivia Blake and her brother, **Reverend**[1] Blake."

"I see. And the **deceased**[2]?"

"Our butler, Edmund. A good man. Very **capable**[3]. He has been with us for nearly ten years now."

"And there was no one else in the house this evening?"

"No."

"I see. Then I must ask you all to inform me of exactly where you were when you heard the scream."

"What? You don't think any of us are involved, do you?" asked Olivia, a **plain**[4] young woman with brown hair and glasses.

"It's **procedure**[5]."

"Well, I can tell you where I was," said the reverend. "In the dining room finishing my brandy. The lights went out, and then there was a scream."

"I see."

"And I was in my bedroom changing my dress," Mrs Grey said. "I had spilled some wine on it during dinner."

"Oh yes, I remember you saying that. I was actually in here. I was looking for the **chess board**[6] so that Alexander and I could play," said Mr Grey, and he smiled at the younger man.

"Yes, and I was in the **study**[7]. I wanted to finish a poem I had been thinking about. I'm a poet, you see?" Alexander said.

1 **reverend** - *Pastor*
2 **deceased** - *Verstorbene(r)*
3 **capable** - *tüchtig*
4 **plain** - *unscheinbar*
5 **procedure** - *Standardprozedur*
6 **chess board** - *Schachbrett*
7 **study** - *Arbeitszimmer*

"And Miss Blake?"

"Well, I think, yes, I was in the hall. I was about to enter the conservatory when the lights went out, and I heard the scream."

Harp shook his head. "So you were all in different parts of the house. And none of you can confirm the **location**[1] of anyone else."

"Do we have to? Don't you believe us?" Mrs Grey asked.

Harp was about to respond when Sloane opened the door, and Harp went to speak to him. "The station just called on the radio, sir. They need me to help with the accident on the old road. I should be back here in an hour."

"That's fine. Everything is under control here," he said, and after a moment he heard Sloane leave the manor house and the sound of his police car driving out into the storm.

He was about to continue questioning the guests when he remembered the file that the cook had given him, and he put it down on a table and opened it.

The first thing he saw was a picture of two men in bed together. One of the men was tall with white hair, and **although**[2] his face was **hidden**[3], he knew it was the owner of Heartfelt. The other was the young writer Alexander Pine.

He looked up quickly, but Mr Grey and his guests were talking quietly and not looking in his direction. He turned the page and saw a picture of an attractive blonde entering a pharmacy, and behind it were copies of prescriptions for a **multitude**[4] of strange **drugs**[5].

He turned the page again and saw a picture of Miss Blake in the street, and some distance in front of her was the same young man who had been in the picture with Mr Grey, Alexander Pine. In fact, there were more than ten pictures of Miss Blake,

1 **location** - *Stelle*
2 **although** - *obgleich*
3 **hidden** - *versteckt*
4 **multitude** - *Vielzahl*
5 **drug** - *Medikament*

and in all of them she seemed to be following the young writer, with a strange expression of **devotion**[1] on her face.

Finally, there was a newspaper article about a **hit-and-run accident**[2], and behind the article there was a picture of Reverend Blake standing next to a car with two broken lights and something that was maybe red paint or maybe blood on the **number plate**[3].

Alibi and motive.

An affair.

A woman with a drug problem.

A stalker.

And a respectable man possibly **guilty**[4] of a hit and run.

Good God, there was evidence in here to suspect that each person in the room had a motive to kill the butler.

He remembered the scene of the murder. The extinguished fire, the destroyed papers.

Had the butler met with one of these people in the library? Was he **blackmailing**[5] one of them? Had that person tried to burn the papers? Had the butler tried to extinguish the fire? Then, in the darkness of the power cut, had that same person taken one of the letter openers and killed him?

Harp was sure that his suspicions were right.

But who was it?

He looked up, suddenly aware that the room was silent, and saw that the five suspects were watching him.

"What is that?" asked the reverend, his voice dangerously quiet.

"I think you know what this is," Harp said. "In fact, I think maybe you all know what this is."

1 **devotion** - *Ergebenheit*
2 **hit-and-run accident** - *Unfall mit Fahrerflucht*
3 **number plate** - *Nummernschild*
4 **guilty** - *schuldig*
5 **to blackmail sb.** - *jdn. erpressen*

There was the sound of thunder outside, and the lights **flickered**[1] for a moment.

"Why don't you give that to me?" Mr Grey said, and he began to walk forwards.

"This is evidence. This means each one of you had a motive to kill the butler."

"Yes," said Miss Blake, who was also now approaching Harp. "But if you think about it, doesn't that also mean that we have a motive to kill you?" And now Alexander Pine and Mrs Grey were also **edging forward**[2].

Detective Harp suddenly understood. He could see it now, in their eyes, in all of their eyes.

He was about to tell them to stop, to keep away from him, but there was the sound of thunder again, and the lights flickered, and then there was complete darkness.

And then there was another scream in Heartfelt Manor.

1 **to flicker** - *flimmern*
2 **to edge forward** - *sich langsam vorwärtsbewegen*

→ The **Lake District** ist ein Ort natürlicher Schönheit und liegt in der Grafschaft Cumbria, im Nordwesten Englands. Der Bezirk ist einer der 14 Nationalparks des Vereinigten Königreichs und kann nicht nur mit dem höchsten Berg Englands aufwarten, dem Scafell Pike, sondern auch mit dem tiefsten See (Wastwater) und dem längsten See (Windermere). Die Briten assoziieren diese Gegend mit deren Dichtern und Literaten aus dem frühen 19. Jahrhundert, wie z.B. William Wordsworth. Die Gegend ist aber auch für die Schafszucht bekannt, die neben dem Tourismus die wichtigste Einkommensquelle darstellt.

16. MURDER IN THE MOONLIGHT

Tony Ricca awoke with a short scream and slapped his naked leg. There was something small and hard on it, but in the pale moonlight that came in through his open window, he could not see what. Perhaps a **cockroach**[1], or some other insect found in the British Virgin Islands. He hit out again and heard the horrible thing fall to his bedroom floor.

He **stretched out**[2], **rubbed**[3] the skin of his leg and was suddenly sure that there was something wrong.

Outside he could hear the gentle sounds of the Caribbean: the **crickets**[4] in the grass, the occasional car on the distant roads.

Yet his villa was silent, and for some reason this made Tony nervous.

For nearly eleven years he had lived here in Paradise, the name he had given his villa, and at some point in the last six years he had begun to relax. He still had his bodyguards to keep him safe: they walked the walls at night and watched his back in the day. But he no longer slept with his gun under his pillow or worried that Don Leone and his men were coming for him.

Until now.

The villa was silent.

Too silent. Where were the footsteps of his guards on the walls? Their **whispers**[5] as they shared a joke in the night? The occasional **growl**[6] of the dogs in the courtyard?

1 **cockroach** - *Kakerlake*
2 **to stretch out** - *sich ausstrecken*
3 **to rub** - *reiben*
4 **cricket** - *Grille*
5 **whisper** - *Flüstern*
6 **growl** - *Knurren*

No, something was not right, he thought, and he moved his hand towards the light on his **bedside table**[1].

"Don't," a quiet voice said, and Tony felt his heart **tighten**[2] with fear.

In the darkest corner of his room, he heard the metallic click of a lighter, and suddenly there was a flame. Tony saw the face of a man lighting a cigarette, his features **distorted**[3] in the shadows. Then darkness returned; the only light now visible was the warm orange **glow**[4] at the end of the cigarette and the pale moonlight from the window.

Tony wanted to shout, but he knew he must not. He did not recognise the face of the man, but he knew that it must be one of his old **acquaintances**[5] and that waiting and talking were his only chance to see another **sunrise**[6]. He had money he could use to buy his life. A lot of money. More than most people could imagine.

And then there was the gun. It was not under his pillow any more, but it was not far away; in the drawer of his bedside table.

"Who are you?"

The silent figure did not speak, but Tony saw the glow of the cigarette move, and he knew that the man had made himself comfortable in the armchair.

"Well? Why are you here? What do you want? There are three men outside: **all I need to do is shout**[7]."

There was the sound of the man **taking** a long **drag**[8] on the cigarette. "No, there aren't," the figure said, and Tony knew immediately that it was true.

"Did you kill them? Or pay them?"

1 **bedside table** - *Nachttisch*
2 **to tighten** - *zusammenziehen*
3 **distorted** - *verzerrt*
4 **glow** - *Glühen*
5 **acquaintance** - *Bekanntschaft*
6 **sunrise** - *Sonnenaufgang*
7 **all I need to do is shout** - *ich brauche nur zu schreien*
8 **to take a drag** - *(von einer Zigarette) einen Zug nehmen*

"**Neither**[1]. They're asleep. Your dogs too. A deep, deep sleep. But they will awake in the morning." And the words were said in such a gentle tone that Tony felt a shiver of fear.

"What do you want? Are you here to kill me?"

Did he have a gun? The way the man spoke made him think that he must have one.

"You don't remember me, do you?"

"What? Well how can I? Let me see your face."

There was silence. "Perhaps I will when I finish this cigarette." Tony tried to think. The man's accent was from Chicago, he was sure of that, but there was no trace of Italian there, nothing to make Tony think he was part of **the Mob**[2].

But he had to be. For eleven years Tony had waited for some **wiseguy**[3] to find him, to finally **get revenge**[4] for the way he had handed the old **family**[5] over to the cops.

"Look, Chicago... That was a long time ago. I had to do what I did. The cops had me, and they knew everything about that fire in the old factory. They said some people got hurt in the apartments next to it and that I would **get life**[6] unless I helped them. You've got to believe me. They knew everything anyway. They were going to take the old family with or without me." Tony did not like the taste of the words in his mouth. The Mob had felt like a real family to him, and it was only the **threat**[7] of life in jail that had made him **betray**[8] them.

"Was it Don Leone? Did he send you? Look, the Don is rich, but I'm richer. I made a lot of money after Leone's men were sent down. Look at me, look at this place. I've got twice what

1 **Neither.** - *Weder noch.*
2 **the Mob** - *die amerikanisch-italienische Mafia*
3 **wiseguy** *(AE)* - *Gangster von der Mafia*
4 **to get revenge** - *sich rächen*
5 **the family** - *die „Familie": amerikanisch-italienische Mafia*
6 **to get life** - *lebenslänglich bekommen*
7 **threat** - *Bedrohung*
8 **to betray sb.** - *jdn. verraten*

he has. So what's he paying you? Because whatever it is, I can double it."

Tony tried to **sit up**[1], but he was suddenly aware of a pain in his leg, and he stretched out to rub it.

The figure in the dark took another long drag on the cigarette. "You know, Leone said almost exactly the same thing. He thought it was you who had sent me. He was an old man when I went to him. He still spoke like a Don though. At least at first."

"You... Leone, you...?" Tony did not believe it: everyone always said the Don was impossible to kill.

"Why did you call your villa Paradise, Tony? Do you really think you will ever see that place? A man like you?" The cigarette **hissed**[2] in the dark, and Tony felt afraid now, but he felt something else too. The pain in his leg was worse, the sensation like a burning in his blood, and it seemed to be moving up his body, making his stomach feel **uneasy**[3].

The gun: think about the gun. You only need a moment. Keep him talking. You have time.

"Did you really kill Leone?"

"Me? No. Killing is for animals."

"So he's not dead?"

"Oh, he is. He died quickly and in pain. For a while he did not even realise he was dying. How do you feel, Tony?"

"What?" And now he could feel it. Something in his stomach. Something in his body. He tried to move, but his legs felt heavy and useless. "What have you done to me?"

The light of the cigarette burnt again. "Me? Nothing."

The gun. Get the gun. Shoot him.

There was a gentle laugh, and Tony saw the figure rise and walk to the window, the cigarette still burning slowly in his hand.

1 **to sit up** - *sich aufsetzen*
2 **to hiss** - *zischen*
3 **uneasy** - *mulmig*

In the pale moonlight Tony could now see the man's face. There was a horrible **scar**[1] on his cheek that went around his mouth and up to his eyes, and there was no hair on the left side of his head.

"Who are you?" Tony asked again, but he thought that maybe he knew now.

"I saw you **testify**[2] against Leone. I was waiting for revenge, but I never found it. The police never gave it to me. They sent your boss, the one who told you to burn the factory, to jail, but that wasn't enough. And they gave you your freedom: freedom to hide here."

For a moment there was silence, apart from the gentle sound of the waves outside and the steady hum of the crickets.

"I never found my revenge, until now. I discovered your villa a year ago. **I could have killed you then**[3], but I needed to decide how. Sally died in a very bad way, screaming as the flames took her. I wanted your death to be like hers." "Sally?" Tony tried to move his hand to the drawer where the gun was, but his arms felt useless, and the pain in his leg was growing. "I don't know what you mean… I…"

"Yes you do," the figure said, and the scarred figure turned.

Tony tried to **roll over**[4], but now the burning pain was in his chest and his arms. "What have you done to me?" he screamed.

The figure turned. "First tell me what you did."

Tony **hesitated**[5], but only for a moment as the pain was too much. "Okay! The factory, the fire. But, I just did what Leone told me. I didn't know anyone would get hurt."

"But they did!" the figure shouted, and he stepped forward, his eyes full of anger. "Sally! My wife! We lived in the apartment next to the factory. I couldn't save her. You animals killed her!"

1 **scar** – *Narbe*
2 **to testify** – *aussagen*
3 **I could have killed you then.** – *Ich hätte dich dann umbringen können.*
4 **to roll over** – *sich umdrehen*
5 **to hesitate** – *zögern*

And the figure raised his hand, and for a moment Tony thought he was going to hit him.

Instead the figure held up the cigarette, which was almost finished. "Look Tony, no more time," he said and dropped it on the floor.

"What do you mean no more time?" Tony asked, but then the pain seemed to reach his heart, and he screamed. "It's burning! Help me! It's burning!"

The figure laughed gently and picked something up from the floor.

"What... what is that? What have you done to me?" Tony shouted.

The figure held up the strange shell, and Tony saw something wet **retreat**[1] inside. "For a year I sat and watched you Tony, thinking about how to get my revenge. Then, one day I heard of a man who was killed by one of these. Its proper name is '**Conus geographus**'[2], and it's a type of **snail**[3]. It's an animal, like you. And a killer. Like you. It has a single tooth in its head, and it uses it to kill fish. It paralyses them and the **venom**[4] burns inside them, and then within a few minutes they die."

"Help me... I have money... hospital, please!" Tony tried to say.

"Too late, Tony. Do you know what some people call this creature? The 'cigarette snail.' Do you know why? Because after it bites you have just enough time to smoke a cigarette before you die," the figure said, and he looked once more at the now **motionless**[5] Tony Ricca. "So I smoked it for you."

1 **to retreat** - *sich zurückziehen*
2 **Conus geographus** - *Landkartenkegel*
3 **snail** - *Schnecke*
4 **venom** - *Gift*
5 **motionless** - *regungslos*

→ Die Britischen Jungferninseln (**British Virgin Islands**) sind ein britisches Überseegebiet in der Karibik. Die offizielle Sprache der über 60 Inseln ist Englisch. Bis auf die Insel Anegada handelt es sich um Vulkaninseln, wo ein tropisches und feuchtes Klima vorherrscht. Bereits seit dem 1. Jahrhundert v.Chr. sind die Inseln von den Arawak bewohnt. Nachdem Christoph Kolumbus die Inseln 1493 für die Europäer entdeckte, begann ein jahrhundertelanger Kampf, der schließlich 1672 mit der Annektierung durch England endete. Damals konzentrierten sich die Engländer auf den Zuckerrohrbau, zu dessen Zweck sie zahlreiche Sklaven schwarzafrikanischer Herkunft einfuhren. Bis heute ist der Großteil der Bevölkerung afrikanischer Abstammung.

17. THE END OF THE LINE

"You've got about two minutes to explain to me what the hell you're doing in my house, and then, if I don't like the answer, I'm gonna shoot you in the head. Does that sound fair enough to you?"

Liz was on the floor, and the rifle of the woman was pointing directly at her.

She could lie, she knew, but if she was about to die in this cold, **damp**[1] cellar, she wanted her last words to be the truth.

"Okay, but can I stand?"

The woman, who was tall and **broad**[2], laughed. "You stand up, and I shoot. You try anything stupid, and I shoot. Now talk."

Liz nodded.

It was a short story, and simple.

"I work for the phone company. I repair the lines when there's a problem. I work all over the Northern Territory, from Katherine to Nhulunbuy to here at Roper Bar. The main office is back in Darwin. Look, I have a business card." She started to look in the pockets of her brown khaki uniform, but the woman shook her head. "Just keep your hands where I can see them."

Liz stopped searching, but she knew now that her screwdriver was still in her pocket. She knew that she had a weapon to defend herself with.

"The storm a couple of days ago caused problems with **heaps**[3] of phone lines. For the last couple of days my partner and I were driving all over the place trying to repair them."

1 **damp** - *feucht*
2 **broad** - *breit gebaut*
3 **heaps of sth.** *(ugs.)* - *ein ganzer Haufen einer Sache, sehr viele*

"Your partner? You got someone else here?"

"No, he hurt his hand last night. He drove back to Katherine this morning to see a **quack**[1]. I've been working by myself all day. Then, about an hour ago, I was thirty miles down the road. There's a section where a couple of telephone lines meet, and it was a bloody **mess**[2] after the storm. I was on the ladder for two hours, and it was getting dark. I knew I had to finish for the night, but I wanted to see if everything was working."

Liz moved a little, just enough so that she could more easily reach the screwdriver.

She wondered if her leg was okay. The woman had hit her on the back of the head, and she had fallen. There was blood on her left knee, but she thought she could probably stand on it.

"Keep talking!" the woman said.

"I attached the **handset**[3] to the line. I wanted to see if I could connect to Roper Bar, but there was nothing. A dead line we call it. So I used my screwdriver to move it around, and that's when I heard it."

"Heard what?"

"Don't you know?"

"**How the hell would I know**[4]? Don't play games with me."

Liz watched her carefully: **either** she was telling the truth, **or**[5] she was very good at lying.

"I heard a kid's voice. A little boy."

The woman's eyes **narrowed**[6].

"He was talking quietly, like he wanted someone in the building not to hear him. He was asking for someone to help him: for someone to call the police. He said his name was Jacky, and he didn't know where he was. He said that someone had

1 **quack** *(AUS, ugs.)* - *Arzt*
2 **mess** - *Durcheinander*
3 **handset** - *Hörer*
4 **How the hell would I know?** *(ugs.)* - *Woher zum Teufel soll ich das wissen?*
5 **either... or** - *entweder... oder*
6 **to narrow** - *sich verengen*

taken him and that he wanted his mum. I tried to speak to him, but he couldn't hear me."

Liz stopped talking.

If this woman had taken the little boy, if she was the kidnapper, then she would probably shoot her now. And if that was going to happen, Liz did not want to be lying on the floor when she died.

"I'm going to stand up now, but I'm not going to move, so don't shoot me, alright?"

The woman did not say anything as Liz rose, but neither did she shoot.

"I don't know what kind of story you're telling, but I don't see how it answers the question of what you're doing in my bloody cellar."

"I didn't know where the call was coming from. All I knew was that it had to be from the north, because the line to the south was dead. I didn't know what to do. Maybe I should have gone for the cops, but I didn't. I got in my truck, and I followed the telephone lines. I passed three other houses; all were empty. Then I got here, and I saw the lights. I looked at my map, and you know what? This is the last house. After this, there's nowhere to go. So I saw the cellar window, and I climbed in."

The woman seemed to move the gun in her hand. Liz thought it was her last chance, and she was about to reach for the screwdriver when the woman spoke.

"You broke into my house, into my cellar, because you thought there was some kid in here? That I was some kind of criminal?"

"Yeah. And that's when you hit me on the head and started pointing that gun at me."

For a second there was silence in the cellar. The woman looked angry but uncertain too.

"Jesus," she said. "I think you're telling the bloody truth." And she lowered the gun.

Liz felt her legs go weak. "You mean, the kid, he's not..?"

"Of course he's not bloody here. But if some **sicko**[1] has got a little kid somewhere, we need to call the cops, now!"

Liz shook her head. "The line's dead, I told you. There's nothing I can do to repair it."

"**Christ!**[2] Then we drive for help. Ropers Bar is small. There's no **cop shop**[3], but we can tell the locals to send someone to Katherine for the police. Get a **search party**[4] out to look. Come on!"

"What's your name?" Liz asked as she quickly followed the woman up the stairs.

"Bess," the woman said and stopped near the front door. "And look, I'm bloody sorry that I hit you, but you were in my bloody cellar like some sort of thief."

"It's okay. I would do the same thing if I was alone out here in the middle of nowhere."

"Yeah," Bess said as they stepped out into the dark. Then she stopped and turned to Liz with a strange expression on her face. "What did you say before?"

"What? When?"

Bess looked north. "**Struth!**[5] You said that the call came from the north, that you looked on the map and that this was the last house. That there was nowhere else to go."

"This *is* the last house."

"Yeah, on the map maybe, but there *is* another place! An old telegraph building, and the phone line connects to it."

"How far?"

"Ten minutes down the road, and then up the old track. Come on! We can take my truck."

The drive was fast and dangerous, and Bess drove like someone who knew that something terrible was about to

1 **sicko** *(ugs.)* - *Geistesgestörte(r)*
2 **Christ!** *(ugs.)* - *Um Gottes willen!*
3 **cop shop** *(AUS, ugs.)* - *Polizeiwache*
4 **search party** - *Suchtrupp*
5 **Struth!** *(AUS, ugs.)* - *Mensch!*

happen. "That poor kid," she kept repeating. "If someone has hurt a kid, I'll bloody kill them!"

Finally they reached an old **abandoned**[1] building, and Bess stopped.

"Did you see that?" Bess asked. "I think I saw a light in the upstairs window.

Liz looked up, but saw nothing.

"Come on!" Bess said **urgently**[2]. "We need to find that kid. You go in the front; I'll go round the back." Then Bess looked at her. "Do you have anything? A weapon? I mean, the kidnapper could still be there."

For some reason Liz thought about lying for a moment: there was a strange feeling in her stomach – a doubt. But then she took the screwdriver from her pocket and showed it to Bess.

"Well, it's not much, but it's something. If you see anyone; if you need help, just shout and I'll be there."

They got out of the car and without another word Bess disappeared into the darkness.

Liz was alone, the empty telegraph building in front of her, the screwdriver in her hand.

Everything was happening so quickly.

Was it doubt in her stomach, or just fear?

She walked quietly to the door of the building and pushed it open. Inside it was silent and dark, but she could smell matches or candles in the air.

She pulled a small torch from her belt and **shone it around**[3]. There was no one there, but in the corner of the room there was a broken telephone on the floor.

This is the place, she knew, and she turned the torch to the stairs and slowly began to walk up them.

She had reached the final step when she heard it.

1 **abandoned** - *verlassen*
2 **urgently** - *dringend*
3 **to shine the torch around** - *mit der Taschenlampe die Gegend ableuchten*

A **slight**[1] sound. Something **muted**[2] and almost impossible to hear.

Bess had told her to shout, but what if there was someone else in the house?

Or what if Bess was the person who had taken the boy? What if everything she had said was to get her here to this dark, empty place?

She turned to her left. In the darkness she could see a closed door, and it looked like someone had very recently been through it.

She took the screwdriver in her hand and pushed open the door.

The room was black, and it was almost impossible to see, but there, in the middle of the room, **illuminated**[3] by the moonlight, was a small boy tied to a chair.

He was kicking his feet and trying to shout, but there was a **gag**[4] in his mouth. For only a second Liz hesitated, and then she ran into the darkness.

She had almost removed the gag when she heard the noise behind her, and she saw Bess standing in the doorway, the rifle in her hand.

"Help me!" Liz shouted.

But the other woman did not step into the room.

She raised the rifle.

Liz saw the crazy, angry look in the other woman's eyes.

No! She thought, but she had no time to speak.

The sound of the shot exploded in the darkness.

For a second Liz did not know what had happened. She could not hear, her ears filled with the sound of the explosion.

1 **slight** - *kaum vernehmbar*
2 **muted** - *gedämpft*
3 **illuminated** - *erhellt*
4 **gag** - *Knebel*

But then Bess put a hand on her shoulder, and she saw the other woman point to the body of the man who had been standing in the dark behind the chair. His dead hand was still holding a sharp knife.

Bess nodded her head and smiled. "Told you I'd bloody kill him," was all she said.

Das **Northern Territory** macht mit 224.800 Einwohnern ungefähr ein Prozent der Landesbevölkerung Australiens aus. Die meisten der hier ansässigen Australier leben in der Stadt Darwin, gefolgt von Palmerston und Alice Springs. In diesen drei Städten zusammen leben 80% der Einwohner dieser dünn besiedelten Gegend. Ca. 29% der Bevölkerung besteht aus Ureinwohnern, die seit über 40.000 Jahren hier angesiedelt sind.

18. THE FUNERAL

"Thanks for coming with me," Mark said as they left the city of Sunnyvale. They were following the other cars along the quiet roads that led to the countryside.

"That's okay," Holly said. "I know he meant a lot to you."

Mark nodded. "Yeah, he was a good man."

The car was hot, and she opened the window, but the warm Californian **breeze**[1] did not cool her much.

"How far is it?"

Mark pointed to a sign. "About fifteen miles."

There was silence for a moment as Holly enjoyed the feeling of the wind in her short black hair.

"I like your family: they seem nice," she said, thinking about the different people she had met at the **funeral**[2].

Mark's mother and father had died when he was young, but he had many aunts and uncles and many, many more cousins.

"Yeah, they are. **Most of**[3] them."

Holly heard the tone in his voice, and she knew that he wanted to say more. They had worked together at the newspaper for almost six years now. He was a good photographer, and she was a good journalist. Now they were good friends, as well as colleagues.

"What is it?"

Mark looked at her, and she could see that he was **troubled**[4].

1 **breeze** - *Brise*
2 **funeral** - *Beerdigung*
3 **most of** - *die meisten*
4 **troubled** - *bekümmert*

"Listen, I know this sounds crazy, but… I don't know. Something about the way he died feels strange. He was always so fit, so healthy."

"He was old, Mark. You said that in the last year he'd been **weak**[1] and tired all the time. I just think that's what happens. It was just old age."

"But he wasn't that old, only seventy-eight. A couple of years ago he was fine and healthy. He used to take long walks near the farm and still **cycled**[2] into town sometimes."

"What did the doctors say?"

"He **refused to**[3] go to the local hospital, but Aunt Mary made him let the local doctor see him. He visited him maybe six or seven times."

"And?"

"He said what you say: old age. He said Uncle Emit's **respiratory system**[4] was weak, but there was no cancer, nothing like that."

Holly considered it for a while. She trusted Mark's instincts almost as much as she trusted her own. However, he was **upset**[5] about the death of his favourite uncle. Probably that was **affecting**[6] his thoughts.

They drove the rest of the way in friendly silence, and after a while they moved from the main road to a small track.

"Here we are" Mark said, and Holly looked up and saw a beautiful white farmhouse on a small hill.

"It's **lovely**[7]."

"Apricot Farm. It's been in my family for generations. Some of my happiest memories are the summers I spent here."

1 **weak** - *schwach*
2 **to cycle** - *Rad fahren*
3 **to refuse to** - *sich weigern*
4 **respiratory system** - *Atmungssystem*
5 **upset** - *bestürzt*
6 **to affect** - *beeinflussen*
7 **lovely** - *entzückend*

They parked the car next to the many other cars in the **driveway**[1] and got out.

Holly stopped for a moment and looked up at the three trees near to the garden. "Are these the apricot trees?"

"Yeah. Years ago there were hundreds, but my **ancestors**[2] started to **grow**[3] **wheat**[4] instead, and now those are the only three."

Holly nodded. "Where are the apricots?"

Mark **shrugged**[5]. "Maybe it was a bad year. Come on, let's go in."

The house was **crowded**[6] and hot. The family and friends were all talking quietly in their black suits and dresses.

Holly recognised many of the faces but remembered few of the names. An **elderly**[7] woman with grey hair was offering drinks to the guests, and Holly knew this was Mark's aunt, Mary. Standing next to the buffet were two cousins who Holly had spoken to earlier. Other people smiled sadly at Mark, and Holly nodded **politely**[8].

For a few minutes they talked to different people, and she was happy to see that Mark was less troubled.

Then a deep voice from behind them spoke, and she saw her friend's face lose its colour.

"Mark?"

"Uncle Pete," he said, and they turned to see a tall elderly man with a white and black beard. "I didn't know you were coming."

"He was my brother."

"Really? And when did you last see him? Did you even know that he was ill?"

1 **driveway** – *Einfahrt*
2 **ancestor** – *Vorfahr*
3 **to grow sth.** – *etw. anbauen*
4 **wheat** – *Weizen*
5 **to shrug** – *mit den Achseln zucken*
6 **crowded** – *voller Menschen*
7 **elderly** – *älter*
8 **politely** – *höflich*

His uncle nodded. "You're angry. You're just like him, you know." Then he paused again. "Emit and I hadn't spoken for many years, Mark, but that was only because he didn't want to speak to me. We had a stupid **argument**[1], and he never accepted my **apology**[2]. But he was my brother."

And the older man moved away to speak to someone else.

Holly looked at Mark and saw the anger on his face. "Mark, what is it?"

"Uncle Pete. Emit didn't like him. They had a business together, but something happened, and they **split**[3] the company." He stopped and thought for a moment. "You know, now Emit is dead, Pete can take control of the **entire**[4] company. He can double his **profits**[5]."

Holly shook her head. "Pete, you're not thinking...?"

"I need some air. Are you okay here?"

Holly nodded and watched Mark leave the room.

For a while she talked to some other guests, but then she walked to the back of the house and out onto the **porch**[6]. She wanted to go look for Mark, when she saw his Aunt Mary arguing with a man with a large stomach at the bottom of the garden. The man seemed worried, and for a while she watched them before she went back into the house.

Thirsty, she went to the kitchen and picked up a glass of water, but it was warm because of the heat.

She looked for the **freezer**[7] but could not see it. At the back of the kitchen, there was a door to the **larder**[8], and she pushed it open and enjoyed the smell of the different foods.

1 **argument** - *Streit*
2 **apology** - *Entschuldigung*
3 **to split** - *aufteilen, spalten*
4 **entire** - *ganz, gesamt*
5 **profit** - *Gewinn*
6 **porch** (*AE*) - *Veranda*
7 **freezer** - *Gefriertruhe*
8 **larder** - *Speisekammer*

The freezer was at the back of the room. She picked up a bag of ice and was about to return to the kitchen when she saw something strange.

It was a large bag of something brown and **flaky**[1]. It almost looked like hard tobacco or **crushed**[2] nuts. Next to the bag there was a hammer and piece of wood that looked like it had been hit many times. Curious, she put some of the brown flakes to her mouth, but discovered that it had a bitter and horrible taste.

She was about to take a picture of the strange stuff, when she heard Mark shouting in the other room, and she ran back through the kitchen.

"Did you do something to him? Did you? In January he was improving, everyone could see that, but then suddenly this summer he gets worse, and no one knows why? Just tell me Pete. Tell me what you did!" Mark was shouting at his uncle, and the other guests were standing in shock.

"Mark," another voice said, and Holly saw the man that Mary had been arguing with. "You have to believe me, it was a **respiratory failure**[3]. Your uncle Pete did nothing."

He must be the doctor, Holly thought.

"Mark, you're upset, but you can't say this sort of thing," Aunt Mary said, and she moved him away from the older man.

Holly followed Mark and his aunt back into the kitchen. "Are you okay, Mark?"

He smiled, but he looked pale and troubled.

"He'll be okay, dear. He just needs a cup of tea."

"Can I help?"

"You sit with him; I'll **put the kettle on**[4]."

For a while she tried to talk to him about something else, but her friend could not forget about his strange ideas.

1 **flaky** - *bröckelig*
2 **to crush** - *mahlen, zerkleinern*
3 **respiratory failure** - *Atemversagen*
4 **to put the kettle on** - *(Tee)wasser aufsetzen*

"Aunt Mary, who gets the farm now that Emit is..."

Mary **frowned**[1]. "Why, dear?"

He shook his head. "Because I need to know that Pete isn't going to live here."

Mary laughed. "Then don't worry. No, Emit changed his **will**[2] a few months ago. He didn't like our brother, and he would never **leave** Apricot Farm **to him**[3]. No, actually, he has left the farm to me, to thank me for helping him this last year."

Mark and Mary continued to speak, but Holly was not listening because she was thinking about an old news story that she had written.

A terrible accident, where a child had been **poisoned**[4].

She turned and looked at the elderly lady making the tea. She watched her take a silver ball with a delicate metal chain attached to it from the cupboard.

"What's that?" she asked quietly.

Mary smiled at her. "A **tea infuser**[5], dear. We only like the best tea in this house. Emit liked his tea."

Holly was silent for a second. "Have you lived here for the past year?"

"Yes. Someone had to take care of Emit. He was very weak at the end."

"But Mark said he got better last winter."

"A little better," Mary agreed, and Holly watched her push the brown tea leaves into the infuser.

Holly turned to Mark and shook her head. "I'm so sorry, Mark," she said, and she saw he was surprised at the emotion on her face.

"It's okay."

"No, it's not. You're right, Emit's death *was* strange."

1 **to frown** - *die Stirn runzeln*
2 **will** - *Testament*
3 **to leave sth. to sb.** - *jdm. etw. hinterlassen*
4 **to poison** - *vergiften*
5 **tea infuser** - *Teeei*

There was silence in the kitchen.

"What do you mean?" Mark asked.

"Do you want to tell him, Mary?"

But the old woman was silent and looked down at the hot water and the silver infuser.

"Mark, your uncle was improving last winter, but only because Mary had no more apricot **kernels**[1] to crush and put into his tea. Then, in spring, when the trees were heavy with fruit again, she continued her work. I don't know how she got the local doctor to lie: I **suppose**[2] she paid him. But I think he knows exactly what it was that **caused**[3] Emit's slow death."

Mark looked at her with an expression of **horror**[4]. "What? What was it?"

"Cyanide, Mark. Apricot kernels contain cyanide."

1 **kernel** - *Kern*
2 **to suppose** - *vermuten*
3 **to cause sth.** - *etw. verursachen*
4 **horror** - *Entsetzen*

→ **Sunnyvale** ist eine Stadt im Silicon Valley und somit Teil der sogenannten San Francisco Bay Area, die sich um die Städte San José und San Francisco erstreckt. Das Silicon Valley ist hauptsächlich als einer der weltweit wichtigsten Standorte der IT und High-Tech Industrie bekannt. Die Branche beschäftigt in Sunnyvale ca. 24.000 Menschen. Das für diese Gegend sehr milde Wetter und die trockenen, heißen Sommer mit Durchschnittstemperaturen von 26 Grad ermöglichen den Anbau von Obst und Wein.

19. THE ESCAPE

Walt was alone in his cell in Auckland Prison's Delta block when he heard the sound of voices in the corridor.

He was no longer a young man, and his dark hair had turned to grey during the past six years in this small space. But his **hearing**[1] was still good and so were his instincts. He could **sense**[2] danger before he saw it, so he moved his hand to his right **boot**[3] and to the short piece of **sharp**[4] wood that he kept there.

"Walt?" a voice called, and the old prisoner recognised the deep, **mocking**[5] tone.

"In here," he said, and he put his hand back on his leg. The voice belonged to a man who could not be stopped by such a small weapon.

Tane stepped into the cell, and Walt took a moment to look at the man. The Maori was massive. Almost too tall to stand in the cell. His shoulders were twice as wide as Walt's and were more heavily muscled than any other man's in Delta block.

But it was the black tattoos on the man's face, head and body that gave him the **menacing**[6] appearance.

That and his dark, psychotic eyes.

"Walt, my old friend."

Walt nodded, but he hated to hear these words in the Maori's mouth. The idea that he could be friends with this murderer made him feel sick.

1 **hearing** - *Hörvermögen*
2 **to sense sth.** - *etw. spüren*
3 **boot** - *Stiefel*
4 **sharp** - *spitz*
5 **mocking** - *spöttisch*
6 **menacing** - *bedrohlich*

"What do you want, Tane?" he said, but he kept the tone of his voice neutral.

Tane smiled, and Walt saw his big white teeth. "I hear that you're leaving us soon."

Walt paused and looked down at the grey stone floor of the cell. "Soon? Yeah. If you think that four years is soon."

"I heard it might be a lot sooner than that, Walt. A lot sooner. Bring him here, Boz."

Boz was Tane's right-hand man, a short, ugly creature with **messy**[1] blond hair.

Boz pushed a man into the cell and followed him in.

"Chris?" Walt said.

"I'm sorry, Walt, they were gonna break my hands: I had to tell them something."

"He was trying to **cheat**[2] at cards again," Tane said.

"It's not true, Walt, I swear."

Walt ignored the young man and looked up at Tane. "So he cheated? Why are you telling me?"

"Because the idiot asked us not to break his hands. He said he had some information for us **instead**[3]."

Walt looked at Chris. He was a tall, thin young man with the face of a boy. People said he was a good thief but that he had met the wrong people and had **got involved in**[4] a bank robbery where a cop had been shot. For two years he had been in Delta block, and for two years Tane had **made his life hell**[5].

"I'm sorry, Walt. They hurt me, my hands…"

"Shut it!" Tane **snapped**[6]. "Boz, watch the door. And **whistle**[7] if you see a guard."

1 **messy** - *unordentlich*
2 **to cheat** - *schummeln*
3 **instead** - *stattdessen*
4 **to get involved in sth.** - *in etw. verwickelt werden*
5 **to make sb.'s life hell** - *jdm. das Leben zur Hölle machen*
6 **to snap at sb.** - *jdn. anfahren*
7 **to whistle** - *pfeifen*

Boz nodded and went to stand in the corridor, and Tane sat down on the chair by the table.

"Now, Walt, you know me. I'm not a bad **bloke**[1]. But I'm a little bit angry with you. I told you that if you ever discovered a way out of this place, you should tell me, and we would go together."

"What did you say, Chris?"

Tane smiled. "So it's true. You told me there was no way out of here."

Walt shook his head. "There is no way out, Tane: this is maximum security."

"But that won't stop you, Walt. How many prisons have you escaped from? Six?"

"Seven. But they were all medium security."

"Yeah, but **I reckon**[2] if anyone can get out of here, it's you. And your stupid **cellmate**[3] tells me you're going to try."

Walt looked into Tane's eyes. The man was a psychopath, but he was not stupid.

If he wanted this to work, he had to be very careful.

"Okay, Tane. There is a way."

Tane **grinned**[4]. "I knew it."

Walt shook his head. "Look, Tane…"

"No, you look, Walt. I don't know what the plan is, but I know this: Boz and I are coming with you, **and that's final**[5]."

Walt waited a moment and then nodded. "Okay, but you have to do everything I say."

Tane nodded. "No worries, old man. You're the expert. So what's the plan. When do we go?"

"Tonight. It has to be tonight."

1 **bloke** - *Typ*
2 **to reckon** - *schätzen, glauben*
3 **cellmate** - *Zellengenosse*
4 **to grin** - *grinsen*
5 **and that's final** - *und dabei bleibt es*

"Jesus, **sweet as**[1]! And the plan?"

"Look, to escape from a prison you need five things: **opportunity**[2], **distraction**[3], **deterrent**[4], delay and an exit strategy. Now, we have the opportunity tonight. One of the guards is leaving, and they are having a party for him at the other side of the prison. That means there are going to be fewer guards than usual."

Tane smiled. "Then?"

"Chris works in the **canteen**[5] in the evenings. He's going to start a fire. That's our distraction. When he does, I know where we can get one of the guard's rifles."

"That's impossible!"

Walt shook his head. "I have a key to the rifle cupboard in the corridor between here and Beta block."

"You have a key? How?"

"The guard that's leaving sold it to me for a small **fortune**[6]. When the fire starts, the guards will enter through that corridor. I'm going to wait near the door and hope they don't see me. There's only going to be five shots, but it's enough to give us some time and space. That's our deterrent."

"You're a bloody genius, Walt. Then what?"

"Delay. When the guards are in the kitchen, Chris is going to get out and block the doors. It won't give us much time, but enough to get to the corridor that leads to the **yard**[7]. From there we climb the first **fence**[8] and get into the exterior space."

"Then what? We can't get over that second fence. It's too high, and there's **razor wire**[9] all over it."

1 **Sweet as!** - *(Neuseeländisch, ugs.) Cool!*
2 **opportunity** - *Gelegenheit*
3 **distraction** - *Ablenkung*
4 **deterrent** - *Abschreckung*
5 **canteen** - *Mensa*
6 **fortune** - *Vermögen*
7 **yard** - *Hof*
8 **fence** - *Zaun*
9 **razor wire** - *Nato-Draht*

Walt let himself smile a little. "Exit strategy. Do you know who Pascal Payet is?"

Tane shook his head.

"In two thousand and one he escaped from a prison in France, and he did it in a stolen helicopter."

Tane looked at him, and Walt saw the doubt in the man's dark eyes. "A helicopter? Are you telling me someone is going to land a helicopter in the exterior yard?"

Walt nodded his head. "An old friend of mine from the army. At eight."

Tane looked at Walt and then at Chris, who was standing silently in the corner with his hands held together.

Then the Maori grinned, his white teeth looking big and dangerous. "Right then. Boz and I are coming with you, so what do you want us to do?"

Walt shook his head. "Everything is planned. If you want to come, meet us at the corridor to the yard at five to eight. Chris can start the fire and block the guards in the canteen, and I can get the gun."

Tane **slapped**[1] his leg and laughed. "You're a genius, Walt, my old friend. You get that gun and give it to me, and I will give us time to get to the helicopter."

Walt nodded.

Outside the door they heard Boz whistle, and they knew the guards were coming.

"Chris," Walt said, "you need to get to the canteen."

Chris moved to the door and tried to smile. "You're not too angry are you, Walt? I had to tell them."

"No, Chris, it's okay," he said, and the young man left the cell.

Tane stood up and was about to leave too.

1 **to slap** - *klatschen*

"Tane, there's a problem. There's only room for three people on the helicopter. More people means too much weight."

Tane looked angry. "Boz and I are coming."

Walt nodded. "I know, but that means that Chris can't."

Tane smiled. "Fine, we don't need that idiot. So, see you at the corridor. And Walt, I don't want any problems, understand?"

Walt smiled too this time. "I think it's all going to go perfectly."

The sound of the prison alarm and the shouting voices **woke** Chris **up**[1]. He was lying on the floor of his cell. The back of his head hurt, and he could not remember exactly what had happened.

Everything had been going perfectly. He had made the fire look like an accident, and in the chaos he had left the canteen and had used three **mop handles**[2] to block the doors.

Then he had met Walt in the cell, and the old **convict**[3] had told him that everything was going to be okay and that they had to leave, and Chris had then moved to the door of the cell.

But then something had hit him.

Something from behind him.

Walt…

It must have been Walt.

The alarm continued to ring, and outside there was the sound of chaos.

The escape. Walt had left him here alone. With no protection from the other prisoners. With no friend and no one to help him. And all because he had told Tane about the plan.

"Walt!" he shouted, but the alarm was so loud he knew no one could hear him.

"Yes?" said a voice.

Chris turned his head.

1 **to wake sb. up** - *jdn. wecken*
2 **mop handle** - *Wischmophalter*
3 **convict** - *Sträfling, Strafgefangene(r)*

Walt was standing by the window of the cell.

"You're still here? What about the escape?"

Walt continued to look out of the window. "The plan is working perfectly. I met Tane and Boz at the corridor. I gave Tane the gun then told him I had to go back to block the door to stop the guards. I told him to wait for me in the exterior yard. That's where they are now."

Chris stood up. "But the helicopter… We have to go!"

From outside in the exterior yard there was the sound of gunshots, shouting and two terrible screams that made Chris jump.

"You know," Walt said, turning around and smiling, "I don't think that helicopter is coming, Chris." And he sat down at the table and opened his book.

Chris looked out of the window at the horrible scene and at the two dead bodies.

And he did not understand.

Das **Paremoremo**, wie das Gefängnis von Auckland auch genannt wird, liegt an der Nordküste Neuseelands und enthält den einzigen Hochsicherheitstrakt des Landes. Im Jahr 1993 schafften es Brian Curtis und Michael Bullock nicht nur aus dem Gefängnis auszubrechen, sondern auch für viele Jahre nicht wieder festgenommen zu werden. Seit diesem Ereignis wurden die Sicherheitsvorkehrungen erheblich verstärkt, sodass die Leitung inzwischen behauptet, es sei jetzt ein Ding der Unmöglichkeit, aus dem Gefängnis zu fliehen.

20. SIX FEET UNDER

The angel was in her dream again; however, this time her steel face was that of an old and angry man. The eyes were filled with hate, and the voice with the sound of **vengeance**[1].

But it was just a dream.

Except this dream seemed to be so much more real than any other. This dream felt cold. This dream was dark. This dream was hard against her back and head.

No, she did not like this dream; so she forced her eyes open.

Normally, her room was light, even at night, because for many years now, she had hated being in places where she could not see. Yet tonight the room was filled with an **impenetrable**[2] darkness, and she felt a sudden stab of fear.

She quickly tried to move her arm to reach the lamp on the bedside cabinet, but instead her elbow **banged**[3] against something hard, and she cried out.

Confused, she tried to sit up, but this time her head **struck**[4] something.

Panic spread over her. The type of panic you feel when you wake in the middle of the night, sweat covering your body, your heart beating, your mind still half-convinced that the monster of the nightmare is a reality.

She kicked her legs, but they too seemed to be trapped. Only then did she begin to form an image in her mind of where she was.

1 **vengeance** - *Rache*
2 **impenetrable** - *undurchdringlich*
3 **to bang against sth.** - *gegen etw. stoßen*
4 **to strike sth.** - *gegen etw. schlagen*

An image of a small space, enclosed on all sides, **virtually**[1] no bigger than the **length**[2] and **width**[3] of a person.

The image of a **coffin**[4].

The sound that escaped from her lips was **horrendous**[5] to hear. It did not sound like a woman at all. It sounded like a **wounded**[6] animal. It sounded like fear itself.

"Help me!" she screamed, her voice muted by the small space. "For God's sake, somebody help me! Help me! There's been a mistake! Get me out of here! Get me the hell out of here!"

After several minutes of screaming and kicking and trying to hit her hands against the wood, she stopped. Slowly she managed to regain some control of herself, to stop the tears that were falling down her face, to slow her breathing and to start thinking.

The first thing she did was check her clothes. They seemed to be the same suit and blouse that she had been wearing when she left the restaurant.

The restaurant. Was that the last thing she could remember? No, she could remember walking home through the city of Newcastle.

So what had happened? An accident?

Despite her fear she was still an intelligent woman. No, there had been no accident. At least, not of the physical kind. The cut on her head was the only part of her that hurt right now.

Right now? What time was it right now?

Her watch, it had **luminous hands**[7]! If she could...

But before she moved her arm, she knew that the watch was not there. For more than ten years she had worn that watch. Now **its very absence**[8] made her begin sobbing again.

1 **virtually** - *praktisch*
2 **length** - *Länge*
3 **width** - *Breite*
4 **coffin** - *Sarg*
5 **horrendous** - *entsetzlich*
6 **wounded** - *verletzt*
7 **luminous hands** - *Leuchtzeiger*
8 **its very absence** - *eben ihre Abwesenheit*

"Damn it, Jean!" she told herself. "**Pull yourself together**[1]. You can get out of this. Think!"

Her watch was gone. That could only mean one thing.

That someone had placed her in this coffin **in spite of the fact**[2] they knew she was still alive.

Her heart began to **race**[3] again, but this time it was anger that drove it. "You cowards!" she screamed.

Her phone? No, if they had taken her watch, they would have certainly taken that.

So she was alone.

Her family would never know what had happened to her, though they would be full of the **suspicions**[4] that had tormented them for years. It was the fear of every judge's family: the fear that one day a criminal would **take revenge**[5] upon the person who had delivered their justice.

In the dark she began to cry again, and this time she made no attempt to stop herself.

"Judge Grey?" a quiet voice whispered. "Can you hear me?"

Judge Jean Grey jumped in shock, her head banging against the wood once more. The voice was quiet and muted, but it seemed to be very near to her. "Who is that? Where are you?" she shouted.

"Judge Grey, if you can hear me, you have to find the walkie-talkie. Can you do that? Can you reach down and find it? Somewhere near to your right leg."

The judge's right hand quickly searched in the dark and found something. It was a thick plastic square, and she could feel large buttons on it.

"Press the first button if you want to speak."

1 **to pull oneself together** – *sich zusammenreißen*
2 **in spite of the fact** – *trotz der Tatsache*
3 **to race** – *pochen*
4 **suspicion** – *Verdacht, Misstrauen*
5 **to take revenge upon sb.** – *sich an jdm. rächen*

For a moment the judge waited. She tried to **compose**[1] herself, to remove the fear and tears from her voice. When she finally pushed the button, it was the voice of the famous **crown-court**[2] judge that spoke. The judge who had brought to justice more criminals than any other in the north of England. The judge who was famous for her tough sentences and iron **rulings**[3]. "Listen to me. Listen very carefully. I don't know who you are. I don't know why you are doing this. I only know that you are making a very big mistake. Do you really believe that you will not be found? I'm a crown-court judge. Someone will have seen you take me. Someone will be looking for you even now. Let the authorities know where I am, and I'll **call for them**[4] to be **lenient**[5]. Fail to alert them, and I'll make sure you suffer for this."

There was a long silence; then the quiet voice spoke again.

"You don't like the dark, do you? You don't like small dark places?"

It was horrible to hear her phobia on the lips of this man, but she was determined to be strong. "What do you want? Money? I have money, but the only way you can get it is to get me out of here now. You may have my wallet, but I'll never tell you the pin code."

"9784," the voice said quietly. "I know all of your secrets, Judge Grey. I know it all. I know where you hide the cigarettes that you tell your husband you don't smoke. I even know why you're scared of the dark, but I want to hear you say it."

The judge's blood turned to ice. This was not the voice of a **petty criminal**[6]. This was the voice of a **madman**[7]. "Look, you

1 **to compose oneself** - *sich zusammennehmen*
2 **crown court** - *Strafgerichtshof*
3 **ruling** - *Richterspruch, Gerichtsentscheid*
4 **to call for sb. to do sth.** - *jdn. auffordern, etw. zu tun*
5 **lenient** - *nachsichtig*
6 **petty criminal** - *Kleinkriminelle(r)*
7 **madman** - *Verrückter*

have to listen to me. I'm a good person. I've done my job for the good of society. If I've sentenced you or one of your family, it was in the name of the law."

Another silence. "Yes, you've been a good person. Not all your life, but for the last fifteen years. Before that, though..."

"So why are you doing this to me?" she shouted.

"Judge Jean Grey," the voice said. And suddenly the judge remembered hearing the voice as she walked past an alley on her way home. She had turned and seen the face of an old man, but then a needle had pressed into her neck, and she had felt herself falling.

"You drugged me!"

"Yes. I learnt all about drugs just for this day. Like I learnt all about you. I watched you. I followed you, for nearly fifteen years. I could have killed you a hundred times. In a way I became you. I became your judge. And this... this is your sentence."

"Who are you?" the judge screamed. And she banged her head against the wood of the coffin and felt **soil**[1] falling between the gaps, soil that made her realise how real this was. How there really was no escape.

"No. Maybe not a judge," the voice said. "Something else. Maybe an angel."

The angel. Every day for fifteen years she had thought about that angel. Every time she had driven past the statue she had tried to look away.

"No. Please, not this."

"Yes, this," the voice hissed. "Fifteen years ago you were leaving your golf club after another extravagant dinner, and you were drunk. You crashed your car on the Durham road, hitting another car and killing the driver. You were trapped in your car, in the dark, alone. I don't know if you could see it: the Angel of the North, the statue looking down on you as you

1 **soil** - *Erde*

cried and begged for **mercy**[1]. I only know that when the family of the dead driver asked for justice from the courts they found none. You used your power and **influence**[2] to cover it all up. You never confessed that it was your fault. The other driver, a young woman, was dead, but you were never punished. Now this is your punishment, Judge Grey."

The judge screamed and shouted and hit her fists against the wood. "I'm sorry! It's true! It's all true. It was my fault. That poor girl. I killed her! God forgive me! But please, don't leave me here! I've tried to make things better, I've tried to be a good person."

When she stopped speaking, there was a quiet sigh, and then the voice spoke for the final time. "That's all I ever wanted to hear you say. Ever since the day you killed my daughter."

For a moment there were no other sounds than the judge's sobbing, but then there was a strange noise above her, and the wood seemed to creak[3].

Tentatively she raised her hands and pushed the **lid**[4] of the coffin, soil and dirt falling into the gaps and covering her. She screamed in fear, fear that the soil would **suffocate**[5] her; then she pushed harder, and this time the lid fell back, and the early morning sky was revealed.

Slowly she tried to stand, her legs weak, and her eyes **unbelieving**[6].

Her coffin was buried in no more than half a foot of soil; the large stone that had been on top of it was lying on the grass.

And the giant statue of the Angel of the North was standing above her, justice and vengeance on her steel face.

1 **mercy** - *Gnade*
2 **influence** - *Einfluss, Beziehungen*
3 **to creak** - *knarren*
4 **lid** - **Deckel**
5 **to suffocate** - *ersticken*
6 **unbelieving** - *ungläubig*

→ Auf einem Hügel in Gateshead, Nordengland, steht seit 1998 die 20 Meter hohe Statue eines Engels. **The Angel of the North**, entworfen von Antony Gormley, besitzt 50 Meter lange Flügel, welche die Statue für Zugreisende auf der Ostküstenhauptlinie zwischen London und Edinburgh sehr deutlich sichtbar machen. Der Künstler sagt über die Statue, dass sie an die Bergarbeiter erinnern soll, die an dieser Stelle über 200 Jahre lang - und in der umliegenden Region mehr als 500 Jahre - in der Dunkelheit gearbeitet haben. Darüber hinaus solle der Engel eine freundliche, beschützende Wirkung ausstrahlen, die durch die Haltung seiner Flügel vermittelt werde: Sie sind leicht nach vorne gewinkelt und deuten eine Umarmung an.

21. CAUGHT RED-HANDED

The body lay on top of the hot red rocks.

It was almost impossible to see that it had once been a person. Now it was only **ruined flesh**[1], broken bones and blood.

The park ranger kneeling in the sand and rock some metres from the mess removed her hat and used it as a fan in front of her face in an attempt to stay cool.

It was no good. It was nearly two o'clock in the afternoon, and the sun was high above the Grand Canyon, its **blistering**[2] rays shining down on the scene.

She looked up at the clear blue sky above the cliffs and shook her head. The fall that had killed the person must have been at least from ten thousand feet, she thought.

“Not a nice way **to go**[3],” she said, quietly, watching the fly that had noticed the body and thinking about what she should do next.

Suddenly, behind her, she heard a footstep. She turned, her hand moving to the pistol on her belt.

“Sorry,” the man said, his face shocked.

He was tall, dark-haired and **disquieting**[4]. Something about the way he stood there made her think that he had been there for some time. That maybe he had wanted to let her know he was there by placing his booted foot heavily on the floor. He was wearing a pair of khaki **pants**,[5] a red and black **lumberjack shirt**[6] and a rucksack that was fastened over his shoulders. He

1 **ruined flesh** - *zerfetztes Fleisch*
2 **blistering** - *glühend*
3 **to go** - *hier: sterben*
4 **disquieting** - *beunruhigend*
5 **pants** *(AE, pl.)* - *Hose*
6 **lumberjack shirt** - *Holzfällerhemd*

looked exactly like the type of hiker that she expected to find out in the canyon at this time of year.

So why did she think he was not what he seemed?

"Who are you?" she inquired, her hand still on the gun.

"Jesus, what… what is that?" he asked.

Ranger Clarke stood up slowly, her eyes carefully **assessing**[1] him from behind her reflective sunglasses. "Do you know what this is? Does it have anything to do with you?" she probed, her tone neutral, yet **beads of sweat**[2] forming on the palm of the hand that was holding the gun.

He shook his head, his eyes never leaving the horrific corpse behind her. "No… no, I… God, is that what I think it is?"

He seemed to have no idea what was going on. Still, there was something about him that she did not quite trust. "What are you doing out here?"

He continued to stare at the bloody mess behind her, and she began to feel her patience disappearing. "Answer me. What are you doing here?" and she unbuttoned the leather **strap**[3] that held her gun in place.

"Hey, what? Look, I'm Zac… Zac Dee, I'm just hiking, you know, the **rim-to-river trek**[4]."

"Have you got any I.D?" she asked.

He nodded, his eyes still on the corpse. "Yeah… I have it here…" and he began to step forwards, but then suddenly he **staggered**[5] and fell.

Despite her **mistrust**[6] she quickly moved to catch him, putting her shoulder under his arm and helping him sit down and remove his rucksack. "You're okay," she said, the same

1 **to assess sb.** - *jdn. mustern*
2 **bead of sweat** - *Schweißperle*
3 **strap** - *Riemen*
4 **rim-to-river trek** - *Wanderung vom Rand des Grand Canyons zum Colorado River*
5 **to stagger** - *schwanken*
6 **mistrust** - *Misstrauen*

words she had said to at least a dozen heat-exhausted hikers. “You need some water.”

He shook his head. “It's not that, it's… God, how can you look at that thing?”

She smiled in spite of the situation. “Not a big fan of blood?”

He shook his head and took the bottle of water from his belt. “I hate it. We should call the police.”

She nodded. “I already did. They should be here in a while. They told me to just wait. So that's what I'm doing.”

“Did you see, you know, what happened?”

“**Nope**[1].”

“It looks like he's fallen right out of the sky.”

She looked around. This part of the canyon was wide, the Colorado River two or three miles to the east. It was not a location that hikers normally came to as they preferred to follow the water.

“People don't just fall from the sky,” she said, **wondering**[2] again if he was who he said.

He looked up. “Sure they do. Parachutes fail to open. People fall out of those little tourist planes. They have those around here, don't they? Maybe there was an accident in one. Or maybe a husband and wife had an argument, and the wife pushed him. Or…”

“Okay, enough,” she said, taking her own water and drinking deeply.

He nodded. “Sorry, I get **talkative**[3] when I'm nervous.”

She thought for a second. “No worries. Look, if you're feeling okay now maybe you should keep moving. I can wait here for the police. There's nothing you can do to help.”

1 **nope** *(ugs.)* - *nö*
2 **to wonder** - *sich fragen*
3 **talkative** - *gesprächig*

He hesitated, and her feeling of mistrust returned. The man claimed that he hated the sight of blood, yet he seemed **in no rush**[1] to get away from the body.

Who was he really?

"I can't just go. I'd feel bad about leaving you. I mean, what if this wasn't an accident. What if there's someone out here watching us right now?"

Watching us right now? Yes, she almost felt like there was. Did he have a friend hidden in the shadows of the rocks, a pair of **binoculars**[2] aimed at her face?

She had to think quickly.

"Don't worry about me," she said, tapping the gun at her waist. "If you want to help, head down to the river and follow it south. You'll probably see the police. Send them in my direction."

He nodded. "Well, if you're sure?" he said, standing up and picking up his rucksack.

She looked around the canyon, her eyes searching for a reflection that meant someone was watching.

There was none.

As he turned back to her, she hesitated for a second. "I'm sure," she said.

Then she pulled her gun from her belt and shot him in the chest.

The sound was not too **deafening**[3] within the canyon, as it was not a high-calibre gun. Still, she had shot him directly in the heart, and he fell back into the dirt without another word.

Shame[4], she thought as she put the gun back. The idiot was just in the wrong place at the wrong time.

1 **to be in no rush** - *es nicht eilig haben*
2 **binoculars (pl.)** - *Fernglas*
3 **deafening** - *ohrenbetäubend*
4 **Shame.** - *Wie schade.*

She turned back to the corpse. She knew what she had to do, although the idea made her stomach **heave**[1].

She took a handkerchief from her pocket and tied it around her face. Then, moving quickly, she walked to the bloody mess then **leant down**[2] and **plunged**[3] her hands into the flesh and guts.

"Jesus Christ!" she protested, her stomach **retching**[4] at the **ghastliness**[5] of the **deed**[6]. "Where is it? Where the hell is it?"

Finally her fingers touched something, and she pulled her hands free, blood dripping from them like paint.

But it didn't matter because she had it. A black plastic tube no bigger than her two largest fingers. It seemed ridiculous that such a small thing could be so expensive, but the Mexican cartel said that it was the prototype of a new drug that would change the world. Stronger than cocaine, purer than opium. Not that she cared about all that. All that mattered to her was the ten million dollars she would receive for taking it to her contact in New York.

She wiped the blood from it with the sleeve of her ranger's uniform, looking with distaste[7] at the stupid green jacket that she had worn for the last eight years.

Had she ever liked the job? Maybe, but not anymore. She wanted a better life than all this. She wanted a house by the ocean, a yacht to relax on and servants to look after her.

She would go back to the Jeep, bring the canister of petrol and burn the two bodies. Then she would go, leave the stupid canyon and never look back.

"Put your hands up, Clarke," a voice said from behind her. She tensed, her hand **hovering**[8] over the gun at her belt.

1 **to heave** - *würgen*
2 **to lean down** - *sich beugen*
3 **to plunge sth. into sth.** - *etw. in etw. hineinstecken*
4 **to retch** - *würgen*
5 **ghastliness** - *Grässlichkeit*
6 **deed** - *Tat*
7 **distaste** - *Abneigung*
8 **to hover** - *schweben*

"Don't even think about it. I don't intend on being shot twice in one day. Turn around."

She raised her hands and turned. He was standing in front of her just like he had been when she first saw him. Except now his rucksack was by his feet, and a gun was in his hand. There was blood on his head from where he had fallen, but none on his chest where she had shot him.

"Yeah," he said with a cold smile. "In spite of your best **efforts**[1], I'm still alive. And now, Caroline Clarke, you're under arrest for receiving drugs with the intention to transport. Also, for **attempted murder**[2]."

"I knew you weren't who you said you were!" she shouted.

"I'm exactly who I said I was: Zac Dee. I just didn't mention that I'm also an FBI agent. We've been watching you for some time, Clarke. We knew the cartel was looking for someone reliable in the States. Looks like they made the wrong choice. I wanted to speak to you, to see if you would work with us to help close down the cartel. But that was before I saw the body and before you attempted to murder me."

In the distance the sound of a helicopter racing across the canyon could be heard. And somewhere near the river was the sound of a police siren. The loose-fitting lumberjack shirt had nicely covered Agent Dee's **bullet-proof vest**[3]. Now it was the **wire**[4] under the same shirt that had done its job.

"No! You can't do this," she said. "You don't understand: they'll kill me. The cartel – they'll find me in prison and kill me."

The cop looked at the bloody mess behind her. "You know, I think you're probably right, but there's not much I can do about that. There's not a judge in the whole country that will

1 **effort** - *Bemühung*
2 **attempted murder** - *versuchter Mord*
3 **bullet-proof vest** - *schusssichere Weste*
4 **wire** - *Wanze (Abhörgerät)*

declare you innocent. You have heard the expression 'caught red-handed', haven't you?"

She looked at her hands. The blood was drying quickly in the sun, and her skin was now the colour of the rocks that surrounded the canyon.

"But tell me," he said, "why this elaborate way of **dropping**[1] the drugs? Who was this? Why did they kill him?"

"I don't know," she said, tears filling the eyes behind her sunglasses. "They just told me to be here. They said they were dropping the stuff today. That it was going to be nicely wrapped so that it wasn't damaged..." She turned back to look at the body one more time. "And that there would be a message reminding me not to make any mistakes."

1 **to drop (off) sth. -** *abliefern*

Grand Canyon, US-Bundesstaat Arizona

Durch den Fluss Colorado in die roten Steine von Arizona geschnitten, ist der **Grand Canyon** als eines der sieben Weltwunder der Natur bekannt. Diese gigantische Schlucht erstreckt sich über 445 km, ist an ihrer schmalsten Stelle 6 km und an ihrer weitesten Stelle 32 km breit. Sie erreicht eine Tiefe von bis zu 1800 m. Je tiefer man in den Canyon hinabsteigt, desto älter wird das Gestein. Während die oberen Schichten erst 270 Millionen Jahre alt sind, entstand das Gestein an den tiefsten Stellen der Schlucht bereits vor 1,84 Milliarden Jahren. Der Nordrand des Canyons befindet sich im Durchschnitt auf 2400 über dem Meeresspiegel, weswegen es hier im Winter schneien kann. Die menschliche Besiedlung dieses Gebiets datiert etwa 12.000 Jahre zurück. Heutzutage teilen sich fünf Völker der Ureinwohner Amerikas das Land um den Canyon: die Paiute, die Havasupai, die Hualapi, die Navajo und die Hopi. Im Jahre 1908 wurde der Grand Canyon zum Nationaldenkmal und 1919 zum Nationalpark erklärt.

22. LIKE FATHER, LIKE SON

"Is he dangerous?" she asked, watching as a guard with a **grim**[1] face emptied her bag onto the table.

For a moment he did not reply, but then he looked up at her with an expression of distaste in his eyes. "This is Folsom Prison, lady: of course he's dangerous."

She felt a knot of anxiety twisting in her stomach, but she tried not to show it.

"Don't listen to him," a younger guard standing by the door to the interview room said. "Old Owen's a teddy bear compared to some of them. He's never any trouble. He does what he's told. You'll be fine."

The first guard turned and looked at the second, his dark eyes angry. "What do you know about him?"

The other shrugged. "He seems okay to me."

"Okay?" The first guard shook his head. "Yeah, well that's because you **don't have a clue**[2] what that sick maniac did." He turned back to her. "But you do, don't you? And now you want to write more stories about him. Did you ever think that the reason these psychopaths do what they do is because of the attention that the newspapers give them?"

"**Leave her alone**[3]," said the other guard. "It's her job."

"Well? Do you know what he did to those children?"

She swallowed and nodded her head. "Yes, but..."

"Yeah, that's what I thought." He put her things back in the bag and passed it to her. "You do not go past the blue line. You

1 **grim** - *düster*
2 **not to have a clue** - *keine Ahnung haben*
3 **to leave sb. alone** - *jdn. in Ruhe lassen*

do not give anything to the prisoner or take anything from the prisoner. You do not take photographs of the prisoner, and any recordings will be copied and given to us. Do you understand?"

"Yes."

He turned to the other guard. "She's all yours," he said then walked away without a second look.

"Ignore him. He's always like that," he said as he opened the door. "There's nothing to worry about. If you want to get out, just shout, I'm right here."

As she stepped into the small white room, she did not know exactly what she was expecting, but the man sitting at the table, his legs **chained**[1] to the floor, and his **wrists**[2] to the table, was not it.

He must have been about fifty years old. His hair was as white as snow, his face lined with worry and **regret**[3], his eyes soft and blue like a summer sky.

Was this really the man she had read about?

"Mr Owen, my name's Julie Cliff. I'm from the Californian Star. Do you know our newspaper?"

The man looked at her for a moment then shook his head. "I don't read the newspapers, Ms Cliff: there's nothing but **misery**[4] in them."

She looked at the chair that had been prepared for her, positioned at the table and behind the blue line that the guard had mentioned. For a moment she hesitated.

"Please, sit down if you like. I don't know what you want from me, but I don't get to see many new faces, so you are welcome." His voice was gentle and polite.

She nodded, walked to the chair and sat down. "Thank you. And thank you for allowing me to speak to you."

1 **chained** - *angekettet*
2 **wrist** - *Handgelenk*
3 **regret** - *Reue*
4 **misery** - *Elend*

He smiled a little. "The **warden**[1] was quite **insistent**[2]. He said he wanted the world to see how his prison could reform a **convict**[3]. Even..." he said letting his eyes look down at his hands. "Even a convict like me."

The small white room was warm, yet his words sent a cold shiver down her back. "I see. Well, maybe the warden has not entirely understood the significance of my visit."

His eyes narrowed a little, and he shook his head. "I won't talk to you about... about things from the past. I've been in this prison for eleven years. I've been **atoning**[4] for those things. You can't ask me about that again," he said, his voice rising a little.

"It's okay, Mr Owen. I don't want to talk to you about that. Not exactly. I would like your help with something."

He stared at her in silence for a moment then nodded. "If I can help, I will."

She took a file from her bag and placed it on the table. "Mr Owen, there have been two crimes committed in the last six months. Very serious crimes. A young man called Daniel Lane and a young woman called Debbie Spencer were killed in Sacramento. Daniel was twenty-two, Debbie twenty. They were both killed in the same way."

"That's... terrible," the convict said. "But how can I help you?"

"You can look at the photos."

There was a strange tension in the room for a moment, **as though**[5] Mr Owen knew exactly what the photos would show.

"Okay, if you think I can help," he said finally, with fear in his soft voice.

1 **warden** - *Gefängnisdirektor(in)*
2 **insistent** - *beharrlich*
3 **convict** - *Sträfling, Strafgefangene(r)*
4 **to atone for sth.** - *für etw. büßen*
5 **as though** - *als ob*

She slowly opened the file, her eyes watching his face and the shock and **disgust**[1] that slowly appeared on it. “Do you see why I think you can help, Mr Owen?”

For a moment Mr Owen was silent, but then a low and horrible **moan**[2] escaped from his lips. “No! No! Not that. Don't show me that!”

The door to the room quickly opened, and the young guard entered. “Is everything okay here?” he asked, his hand moving to the radio at his belt.

“It's okay,” she said.

“It's not okay!” Mr Owen groaned, turning his head away from the pictures. “It's not!”

“Mr Owen, you said that you wanted to help. These people, they're about the same age as your son Billy, aren't they? Don't you want to stop the person who did this? Stop someone hurting people like Billy?”

The sound of his son's name seemed to silence him, and after a moment he nodded, though tears had risen to his eyes.

The guard looked at her **questioningly**[3].

“It's okay,” she said then watched as he left the room and closed the door again. “Mr Owen, I don't want to **upset**[4] you. I've read the reports about your crime. I know that you have always said how sorry you were for what you did.”

“I… I was… I am. It was a terrible thing.”

“The police don't believe me, but I think that there's a **copycat** killer[5] somewhere in Sacramento. Someone who is trying to recreate your crimes. You saw the mouths of the victims. They were… **ripped**[6]. Just like the mouths of the four children… that were found in your basement.”

1 **disgust** - *Ekel*
2 **moan** - *Stöhnen*
3 **questioningly** - *fragend*
4 **to upset sb.** - *jdn. durcheinander bringen*
5 **copycat killer** - *Nachahmungstäter*
6 **ripped** - *zerrissen*

Tears began to fall down Mr Owen's face, but he nodded his head.

"Mr Owen, you never explained why you did that to your victims. I think that maybe if you could tell me that now, it might help the police to find the type of person who committed these horrible crimes. And you want to help, don't you? You want to help the young people like your son?"

"Yes," he said, quietly. "I would do anything for Billy..."

"Does Billy come to visit you, Mr Owen?" she asked, thinking that maybe his son's name would encourage him to speak a little more.

"No," he replied, shaking his head. "No. He lives with a **foster family**[1] in Washington. It's better... better if he's there."

She nodded. "I understand."

He moved his head to look at the pictures one more time, tears still rolling down his face.

"So? Can you tell me why you did that? Why you ripped their mouths?"

When he spoke again his voice was strange and distant. "I don't know... I think...I think the rips made them look like they were... smiling," he said.

"Smiling?" she asked, another cold shiver running down her back.

"Yes, like they were happy. Like it was all just a game."

She was silent for a moment. "Why did you want them to smile?"

He looked at her then, more tears escaping from his gentle eyes. "Everyone needs friends," he replied quietly. Then a scream escaped from his lips, and he began to kick the table and pull at the chains holding his wrists. "Everyone needs friends!"

The door to the interview room opened again, and this time the first guard entered. "That's it! The interview is over."

1 **foster family** – *Pflegefamilie*

"But why, Mr Owen?" she tried to ask, the sound of his screams almost unbearable to hear.

"You've got your story, now get the hell out of here", the guard shouted, pulling her up and pushing her out of the room.

The younger guard came forward and gently took her arm to escort her along the corridor to the exit. "Are you okay?" he asked.

"Yes," she said, her heart beating strongly. "Just... God... I don't know... he seems so fragile. I almost can't believe he could ever do anything so terrible."

"Yeah. I know what you mean."

They reached the next security door and stopped as they waited for it to open. "Does he ever have any visitors? He said he doesn't get to see many new faces."

The guard shook his head. "Not many, just the son. He's been coming every week for the past few months. Strange kid. Quiet. They don't even talk really. It's like the old man can't look at him. The **guilt**[1] I suppose."

She turned to him, a horrible feeling rising in her chest. "The son? Billy? But he's in Washington with his foster family."

"Not anymore. He's twenty-one now. He moved back to Sacramento half a year ago. But like I say, he's a bit strange. I can't imagine he's made many friends."

"What?" she asked as the door opened.

"Yeah, you know, he's a bit **odd**[2]. But then maybe that's what happens when your father is **convicted**[3] of murder."

She stopped before the door, her mind racing, her memory of the old newspaper stories returning to her.

"No," she said. "No, he was always like that. The reports said he didn't say a word as they took his father away. That he never even asked why. He was in the house the day the kids were killed. In his room."

1 **guilt** - *Schuldgefühl*
2 **odd** - *seltsam*
3 **to be convicted of a crime** - *eines Verbrechens überführt werden*

The guard shrugged. "Yeah, well, **like father like son**[1], I suppose."

No, not like father like son, because the father seemed so gentle, so kind. Then Mr Owen's words returned to her. "*I would do anything for Billy...*"

→ 1880 öffnete das **Folsom Prison** 32 km entfernt von Sacramento, Kalifornien. Das Gefängnis wurde besonders durch ein Konzert bekannt, das Johnny Cash 1968 hier für die Gefängnisinsassen veranstaltete. Sein berühmter Song „Folsom Prison Blues" war allerdings schon über ein Jahrzehnt früher entstanden. Folsom Prison ist eines der ersten Hochsicherheitsgefängnisse der Vereinigten Staaten. In seinen Anfangszeiten mussten die Häftlinge 7,5 Stunden am Tag ohne Mittagessen in einem Steinbruch arbeiten. Heute fertigen die Insassen die Kennzeichen aller in Kalifornien zugelassenen Fahrzeuge und stellen Straßenschilder her.

1 **Like father like son.** – *Wie der Vater, so der Sohn.*

23. MURDER WILL OUT

Above the granite-grey mountains of the Scottish Highlands, storm clouds were slowly moving across the dark skies of another cold winter night.

In the deep valleys and quiet towns below, the clouds' approach seemed to bring with it a growing sense of danger. Yet, in an old hunting **lodge**[1] on a quiet road between two silent hills, this **sense of impending doom**[2] was **muted**[3] by drunken voices, laughter and the sound of wine glasses being brought together.

"To us! And to another year of good business," a man of about sixty years with a dark beard and large smiling eyes said. Around the table the other dinner guests raised their glasses.

It was an elegant room. The table was dressed in white cloth, and the light was provided by more than twenty candles placed in delicate silver holders.

"How about another bottle of wine, Hamish?" the man with the dark beard and smiling eyes asked.

At the head of the table, a younger man with a pale face shook his head. "I think it's time for the port, Mac," he said, signalling to the butler who stood silently by the door.

"Good idea!" Mac replied.

"The port please, Bill," Hamish politely said to the elderly butler. "Then you may leave us for the night."

The master of the house and the servant exchanged a long and serious look. "If you are sure, sir?"

1 **lodge** - *Hütte*
2 **sense of impending doom** - *Vernichtungsgefühl*
3 **to mute** - *dämpfen*

Hamish nodded, and the butler moved away, returning with a dusty bottle of port.

"Looks like good stuff," said Duncan, the red-headed man to the left of Hamish.

"It's... special," Hamish replied. Then he watched carefully as the butler took the cork from the bottle and filled the twelve small glasses around the table. "Not yet, Anne," he said, as he saw an attractive middle-aged woman lift the glass to her lips. "I would like to make a toast first."

Hamish watched the butler leave the room and close the large **oak**[1] door. Then he stood, his glass of port in his hand, and he looked around the table.

Duncan, Col, Sandra, Anne, Kevin, Beth, Mac, Pete, Chris, Mike and Sally. Eleven people that he had known for more than ten years. Some of them, like Mac and Kevin, he had known since he was a child. Many of them he had considered part of his family, and all he had considered friends.

But what were they now?

"I would like to make a final toast tonight. You all know me: you all know that I am a man of few words. However, today, as I am sure you all know, is the **anniversary** of my father's **death**[2], and I would like us to raise a glass to him and to wish him peace."

The atmosphere in the room changed so quickly that it seemed like a window had been opened and the storm had been allowed to enter.

"To your father," said Mac.

"Yes, to Douglas, a good friend and a great businessman," said Kevin.

"To Douglas," Anne agreed, and everyone around the table nodded their heads or gave their own quiet **toast**[3].

1 **oak** - *Eiche*
2 **death anniversary** - *Todestag*
3 **toast** - *Trinksrpuch*

Hamish nodded, looked at them, and then drank. Around the table eleven other glasses were lifted to lips, and everyone shared in a moment's silence as they tasted the dark port.

Only when he was sure that everyone there had tasted the rich **fortified wine**[1] did Hamish speak again. And when he spoke, his voice was deeper, louder, more filled with some dark and terrible meaning. "**Murder... will... out**[2]."

The three words hung in the air around the table.

"What?" Kevin finally asked, his normally relaxed expression replaced by uncertainty. "Why would you say that, Hamish?"

Outside, the rain began to fall more heavily, and the wind screamed around the lodge, but inside there was only the **crackle**[3] of the candles and silence as they waited for Hamish to reply.

"Why? You all know that these were the final three words that my father said. You all know that **in this very house**[4] he fell to the floor in his room and died. Some of us were here. Duncan, Col, Sandra, Anne, Mac, Pete. Others had left and were driving home. But only hours before, we had all been here together. When he fell to the floor we heard his screams, and we ran to his room. His face was already blue, his eyes red with blood, but as he lay there on the floor we all saw him raise his hand and point to me, his only son. Then he said those three words, words which I have not stopped thinking about from that day to this. 'Murder... will... out.'"

Mac shook his head. "Yes, we were there; we saw it, but that's all over now. We all know that you had nothing to do with your father's death. We know you loved him."

Hamish nodded. "Yes, you were all very supportive. We told the police what he had said, but you all agreed that it

1 **fortified wine** - *Dessertwein*
2 **Murder will out.** - *Der Täter wird erwischt. / Die Wahrheit wird herauskommen.*
3 **crackle** - *Knistern*
4 **in this very house** - *in ebendiesem Haus*

was a mistake: the dementia of a sick man. But then someone sent a letter to the police. A letter that said I was guilty, that I had planned to kill my father to **inherit**[1] his money and his business."

"A horrible joke. Or some **competitor**[2] trying to ruin the business. We all know that," said Sandra.

"Someone from another oil company. It's obvious," agreed Pete.

"Yes, that's what we thought. So I told the police that I would help them in any way that I could. That they could interview me, search my office, search my home."

"But there was nothing to be found, because you were innocent," said Sally.

Hamish moved from the table to stand at the window. For a moment he watched the rain before turning back to the eleven people. "It's true. There was nothing there when the police searched my home. But that is only because my butler, Bill, found the **poison**[3] that killed my father before the police arrived."

There was a **stunned**[4] silence.

"What do you mean? Your father died of a heart attack," said Anne.

"Yes, Anne, a heart attack caused by a poison."

Kevin stood up and shook his head. "What are you saying? This makes no sense! The doctors found nothing in Douglas's blood."

"That's true, Kevin. However, I believe that was only because the person who killed my father did not know about all of the medication he was taking. One of the **prescribed**[5] drugs hid the poison."

1 **to inherit sth. -** *etw. erben*
2 **competitor -** *Konkurrent(in)*
3 **poison -** *Gift*
4 **stunned -** *verblüfft*
5 **to prescribe -** *verschreiben*

"I don't understand anything you're saying," said Sally. "Why was there poison in your house?"

Hamish sat back down at the table. "Because the killer wanted the police to think that I was guilty. They wanted to **frame**[1] me for my own father's murder. If Bill had not found the poison, I would now be in prison."

"But why would someone do that?"

There was a flash of lightning from the storm outside, and Hamish smiled. "Is it not obvious? Think about my father's last words."

Duncan shook his head. "Murder will out?"

"Yes. I thought he was saying that the guilty person would be discovered. That the crime would be revealed. But I was wrong. My father was a clever man, cleverer than I am. Even in those last moments he knew that if I was found guilty of murder, I would be out of his **will**[2]. Murder… will… out. Out… of his will! He knew that someone had wanted me to lose control of the business… and he knew that it was someone in this room."

Some of the guests stood. "You can't be serious?" asked Mac.

"Oh, but I am. I have never been more serious. I have thought about it for a year. The killer must be one of you. You were all here the night of his murder. Any one of you could have poisoned his drink. And all of you own shares of the business. All of you would be rich if you took control."

The eleven people began to look around at the others' faces. "But who? Who was it?" cried Anne.

"Well, that is the difficult part. But I have a solution. A way of discovering the truth. Bill has locked the doors. None of us may leave until someone has **confessed**[3]."

1 **to frame sb. for sth.** – *jdm. etw. anhängen*
2 **will** – *Testament*
3 **to confess** – *ein Geständnis ablegen*

"What? You're joking?!" shouted Pete, who ran to the door but **failed**[1] to open it. "You're **insane**[2]! No one is going to confess. Let us out!"

"Someone will confess. You see, also, before the meal, Bill and I took the poison that killed my father and injected it through the cork of the bottle of port that we are all drinking. The **antidote**[3] for the poison is outside with Bill. Enough for all of us, including the killer. I only want a confession. I don't want anyone to die."

For a moment there was silence, but then chaos followed. Some of the guests stood up and shook their heads in disbelief; others began to shout and scream at Hamish. Three ran to the door and began to kick and hit it, and Duncan ran to the window and tried to smash the **reinforced glass**[4].

Only two people remained silent and seated. One of them was Hamish; the other was Mac. The older man with the dark beard and usually smiling eyes put his head in his hands and swore.

"What is it, Mac?" asked Hamish, and some of the others turned to look.

"You bloody idiot! You don't know what you've done!" he shouted. "There is no antidote to that poison. You've killed us all!"

Hamish waited silently for all of the other guests to understand the significance of Mac's words; then he raised the glass of port to his mouth and drank. "I know," he said. "But you see, there's no poison in that bottle either."

1 **to fail to do sth.** - *etw. nicht machen können*
2 **insane** - *verrückt*
3 **antidote** - *Gegengift*
4 **reinforced glass** - *drahtverstärktes Glas*

Bohrplattformen, Cromarty, Großbritannien

Zu den schottischen Seegewässern gehören sowohl Teile des Nordatlantiks als auch Teile der **Nordsee**. Die Öl-Ressourcen in der Nordsee vor der schottischen Ostküste gehören zu den größten in der Europäischen Union. Sie wurden in den 1960er Jahren entdeckt; mit der Ölförderung wurde 1976 begonnen. Das plötzliche Wachstum und die Entwicklung der Nordsee-Öl- und Gasindustrie der 1970er und 80er Jahre schaffte tausende neuer Arbeitsplätze und machte Aberdeen und seine Umgebung zu einem der wohlhabendsten Standorte des Vereinigten Königreiches.

In einem Volksentscheid im Jahr 2014 wurden die Bewohner Schottlands befragt, ob Schottland Teil des Vereinigten Königreichs bleiben oder unabhängig werden soll. Die Befürworter der Abspaltung betonten, dass ein unabhängiges Schottland eines der reichsten Länder der Welt wäre, denn der Großteil der Ölfelder liegt in schottischen Gewässern. 55,3 % der Schotten entschieden sich gegen die Abspaltung.

24. MURDER IN THE ICE

The celebration, if that is what it should be called, was slowly coming to an end now.

Most of the younger staff of Fairbanks police station had either gone home or returned to their desks to complete their shift under the warming influence of a large whisky or two. The older staff, however – the ones who had known Ken Hooper since the early days – were standing around a table raising another glass to him.

"To Hooper's retirement! He shot like a girl, drank like a girl, but he sure as hell knew how to **crack a case**[1]!" said Detective Hutch, a big red-headed man with more than a few **streaks**[2] of silver in his beard.

Around the table three other men raised their glasses to Hooper, and the centre of attention, a short balding man with a plain and honest face, nodded his head and raised his own glass. "Thanks for speaking about me in the past tense already, Hutch. It'll be you next, you know."

The men laughed. "Maybe," said Hutch. "But not for a while yet. I'm still **in my prime**[3]. **Speaking of which**[4], if any of you are thinking about going home, I'll get the chief to put you up for retirement too. There's still **many a tale**[5] to be told about old Hooper here."

Hooper shook his head. "I don't know, Hutch. I still have a bit to get sorted out here."

1 **to crack a case** – *einen Fall lösen*
2 **streak** – *Strähne*
3 **to be in one's prime** – *im besten Alter sein*
4 **Speaking of which...** – *Da wir gerade davon reden, ...*
5 **many a tale** – *manch eine Geschichte*

"No problem. Throw your stuff in a box and come meet us over at the Anchor. It's either that or we drag you there now and **cuff you to the bar**[1]," Hutch said with a grin.

"I guess one more won't hurt."

"Ha! One more? Do you see what I mean lads? He drinks like a girl!"

Hooper shook his head with a smile and strolled back to his office as the others pulled on their winter coats and scarves.

Stopping at the door, he looked at the small dark space.

It seemed strange to see it so empty.

He had cleared out his **filing cabinets**[2] and stripped the walls of the usual case files and information that he had so **studiously**[3] collected. Even his plants were gone, sent home with Molly, his wife, two days before.

"Thirty-five years," he said to himself, shaking his head in disbelief. Thirty-five years, and finally it was all over.

Had he ever really expected to make it to retirement? He had certainly faced his fair amount of trouble over the years. Or gone looking for it, as Molly would doubtless say.

Taking the final cardboard box, he moved around the room picking up the last items that he had to collect: an old notepad which had sat at his desk for almost as long as he had, a mug from his son with the words *Best Dad* printed on it, and a picture of himself and the guys ice fishing over in the White Mountains when their faces had been free of lines and their futures stretching out in front of them.

"A million years ago," he muttered, picking up the box.

He looked around the room once more and was about to leave when a long-forgotten memory came to him.

White Mountains.

1 **to (hand)cuff sb. to sth.** - *jdn. mit Handschellen an etw. fesseln*
2 **filing cabinet** - *Aktenschrank*
3 **studiously** - *sorgsam*

Slowly he put the box back down and turned around, looking at the filing cabinet as if it were the first time he had ever seen it.

Was it still there, he asked himself, knowing that the answer was yes.

And do you really want to look at it?

This time no answer appeared.

He walked slowly to the cabinet and pulled open the top drawer. Then, placing his hand under it, he felt for the file which he had placed there so many years earlier.

His heart beginning to beat faster, he took the file back to the desk, turned on the small lamp and sat down. In the station the occasional person passed along the corridor, but he knew they would not disturb him. He was just some old retiring cop **lamenting**[1] over the one case he had never really solved. The one case that had haunted him for years.

The one that had got away.

He opened the file and looked at the **scribbled**[2] notes. It had been a year after the fishing trip when they had received the call.

The report said that a black Jeep had driven past a group of fishermen on the mountain road, attracting their attention because of its speed. The fishermen had claimed that a young woman in the passenger seat of the car had seemingly been **in distress**[3].

Hooper and Hutch had been returning from another case and were the closest to the area. So, despite Hutch wanting to leave it to the uniformed cops to follow up, they had followed the route and had finally found the black Jeep parked in the bushes by an abandoned hunting lodge[4] which was still covered in snow and ice after a long and cold winter.

1 **to lament over sth.** - *über etw. klagen*
2 **to scribble** - *kritzeln*
3 **in distress** - *in der Not*
4 **hunting lodge** - *Jagdhütte*

On seeing the Jeep, Hutch's attitude had seemingly changed from one of complete disinterest to obvious concern.

Exiting their car, they had split up, Hutch taking the front and Hooper moving silently around the back to cover the exit.

Normally they had always worked well together, giving the other enough time to get into position before making a move, communicating properly.

But not that day.

No, that day Hutch seemed to forget it all. He kicked open the door before Hooper could get anywhere near the back entrance.

When Hooper heard the first shot, he dived into the snow and pulled his own gun free. The next shots came quickly, but it was obvious that they were not directed at him so, **scrambling**[1] to the back **porch**[2], he smashed open the door and moved into the room to see the scene of horror.

The young woman was clearly dead.

Her hands and legs were tied to a bed, her clothes torn from her body and a single gunshot wound in her head.

Hutch was at the door, quickly reloading his gun then firing four more shots at the Jeep as it departed along the snow-covered road.

"What happened?" Hooper asked, running to the door as the Jeep disappeared into the trees.

"I was too slow. He must have seen us. I saw him raise the gun. I kicked open the door, but it was too late." Hutch's face was pale behind his red beard.

Hooper looked around the **derelict**[3], half-frozen room. "How did he get past you?"

1 **to scramble** - *hasten*
2 **porch** *(AE)* - *Veranda*
3 **derelict** - *verlassen*

Hutch turned to him, his face suddenly **furious**[1]. "I was too slow, okay? The girl's dead. I was too slow."

Hooper nodded, not understanding where the rage came from. "We'll get him, Hutch," he told his old partner. "Don't worry, we'll get him."

But they never did.

In the empty office all these years later Hooper shook his head and sat back. It was a mystery. The man should have been easy to find. Hutch had not only seen the man's face, but they had also seen the Jeep. Yet, despite these two strong **leads**[2] the culprit had **disappeared into thin air**[3].

After six months of pursuing sightings of black Jeeps or men matching the description, Hutch had asked Hooper to forget about it. He had said that the memory of seeing the girl like that, of thinking how close he had got to saving her, was too much. He had said that he did not want to think about the man's face ever again. That he thought he would never forget that face.

Hooper had never understood, but he had put the case to one side, taping it in the filing cupboard with the intention of studying it alone some time.

"But I forgot," he thought to himself shaking his head. "How did I forget?"

"Anything wrong?" said Hutch, silhouetted in the doorway of the office.

"Hutch. I was just coming."

"Yeah, sure. I knew you'd take your time, so I thought I'd come and drag you over. What's that? Some old case?"

Hooper nodded, unsure of how to begin. "Hutch, can I ask you something? Something about that day in the White Mountain hunting lodge?"

1 **furious** - *zornig*
2 **lead** - *Hinweis*
3 **to disappear into thin air** - *sich in Luft auflösen*

Even in the gloom of the office it was easy to see the colour fade from Hutch's face, the good humour flee from his eyes.

"Tonight? Why?"

Hooper breathed out slowly. "Because you said you would never forget the face of the man who shot that girl. Can you do something for me? Can you describe him to me now?"

Hutch stood as still as a statue in the doorway. "That's the file, isn't it? The damn sketch is in there."

Hooper picked up the file, turned the page and looked. "Yeah, it's here. But I still want you to describe him."

Hutch shook his head. "It was thirty **goddamn**[1] years ago."

"You said you'd never forget that face."

For a moment Hutch was silent. Then he moved into the office and shut the door. "Yes, Hooper. I said I'd never forget the face of the man who shot that girl." Hutch looked straight at Hooper, the confession in his eyes before he even spoke it. "How could I? I see it every day in the goddamn mirror."

To Hooper the words felt like ice piercing his heart, yet he felt he had always suspected the truth. "Why? Hutch? Why did you do it? Who was he? Who was the man you were protecting?"

Hutch breathed out deeply. "My brother. My youngest brother. He was always a piece of rubbish, but when I saw him there… What could I do? I had to help him. If he had been caught, I would have been **disgraced**[2], and he would have rotted in jail. She could have identified us both. I shot her – I had to. I told him to go, to get out of town and never come back. No one could identify him. Nothing could lead back to me."

Hooper shook his head. "The identification was fake. And you didn't really shoot at the Jeep as it drove away. You should have told me, Hutch."

"Why? What would you have done?"

Hooper sighed. "Arrested you, old friend."

1 **goddamn** - *verdammt*
2 **disgraced** - *blamiert*

"I know," Hutch said, removing his pistol from his belt. "You always were the better cop. The better man too."

For a moment Hooper watched the gun in Hutch's hand and saw the conflict in the other man's face.

"You're a better man than you know, Hutch," Hooper said quietly, his eyes in Hutch's eyes.

For a second more Hutch stood there, but then he sighed, placing the gun on Hooper's desk.

"I don't suppose you want a last drink with an old friend, do you?" Hutch asked.

But Hooper shook his head and took his handcuffs from his belt.

Fairbanks, Alaska

Etwa 190 km vom Polarkreis entfernt liegt **Fairbanks**, Amerikas nördlichste und kälteste Stadt. Einst von Goldgräbern gegründet, ist Fairbanks heute bei Wanderern, Kletterern, Jägern und Freizeitfischern beliebt. Jeden Februar in Jahren mit gerader Jahreszahl startet bzw. in Jahren mit ungerader Jahreszahl endet hier der Yukon Quest, eines der härtesten Langstrecken-Schlittenhunderennen der Welt, das sich über 1.600 km in Kanada und Alaska erstreckt.

Wegen der unmittelbaren Nähe zur Sowjetunion wurde in Fairbanks im Zweiten Weltkrieg eine Militärbasis eingerichtet, die auch noch während des Kalten Krieges besetzt war.

Heute gilt Fairbanks als eine der Städte mit der höchsten Verbrechensrate der U.S.A. und steht auf Platz drei der für Frauen gefährlichsten Städte des Landes.

25. NO SMOKE WITHOUT FIRE

In an office on the **outskirts**[1] of Ottawa, a man in dark clothes held up a glass of whisky to a picture on the wall. "**Here's to you**[2], Gavin," he said, before **downing the drink**[3] in a single swallow, the hot liquor burning in his throat.

The picture was of Gavin White, CEO of White Incorporated; the picture was of the man holding the glass of whisky. His hair was a little darker, his face a little less lined, and his eyes were full of an optimism which was no longer there. But it was certainly the same man.

He filled the glass again then stared at his own portrait. How long ago had it been since the picture was taken? Ten years? Twelve?

Everything had been so different back then. His offices had been in the centre of the city, not on these forgotten **perimeters**[4] where there were only start-up businesses and failing companies. He had been a **real player**[5] back then, a name that people mentioned with admiration or envy.

And he had been rich.

Was it the loss of respect that hurt the most, or the loss of the millions that he had once possessed?

He laughed.

It was the money, of course. The rest of it could go to hell. He would trade all the respect in the world to get back half of

1 **outskirts** - *Stadtrand*
2 **Here's to you.** - *Auf dein Wohl.*
3 **to down a drink** - *ein Getränk austrinken*
4 **perimeter** - *Stadtrand*
5 **real player** - *führende Figur*

what he used to have. To own just one of the sports cars or one of the riverside apartments.

Yes, he would do anything to have his bank account full once more. To not have his credit cards declined or his **loan requests**[1] denied.

"You're going to get it all back," he said. "Unless you mess this up, you're going to get it all back!"

He emptied the whisky again then looked at his hand.

It was shaking.

"Be a man, Gavin! Follow the plan and nothing can go wrong."

He was about to pour a third glass, but he stopped himself.

"Later! When you're back at the hotel celebrating, you can drink."

He nodded to himself, put the bottle back in the cabinet under the picture and laid the glass down on his desk.

His plan was simple, yet brilliant.

Seven years ago, when things had started to look bad for the company, he had slowly begun to increase his insurance. He had made sure that no one had known he was losing money for as long as he could. Then he had **downsized**[2] to this smaller office block and waited.

For three years now he had been almost bankrupt, his assets gone, his **stocks**[3] failed. A less intelligent man might have thought of pulling an **insurance job**[4] as soon as things got bad, but Gavin knew that he had to be careful.

He had waited until people had stopped thinking about Gavin White and White Incorporated. He had waited until his now pitiful business seemed to be doing okay.

He had waited until tonight.

1 **loan request** - *Darlehensantrag*
2 **to downsize** - *schrumpfen*
3 **stock** - *Aktie*
4 **to pull an insurance job** - *einen Versicherungsbetrug begehen*

Now he was ready.

Did he care that twenty people would lose their jobs, their salaries? **Did he hell!**[1]

This was his ticket out of here. A ticket to a **condo**[2] in the States, where he could drink away the rest of his life.

But he still had to be clever; he still had to be careful.

He picked up the whisky glass and walked through the dark offices. Outside the stars hung above a cold night in the city, the lights of the capital almost pleasant to look at in the darkness.

He took the glass to the kitchen, washed it then placed it back into the cupboard.

He could leave no trace to let the police know he had been here.

When they checked, they would see that he was staying at a hotel in Quebec City. Two friends would say that he was with them drinking in their hotel room all night. Two friends who would receive a small percentage of the money he would make.

He had left the hotel at midnight and driven back in a rental car then waited in the shadows of the office block.

There had been no one in the area, with only one or two lights on in the apartment block **opposite**[3]. In his dark clothes he had entered the building, the alarm of which he had reported damaged two days before.

So there would be no record of his entrance, no witnesses and a strong alibi to protect him.

"See, Gavin," he said to himself. "You've got this! You can do it."

He walked back to the main office where his employees worked. Fifteen computers were sleeping in the darkness. One, however, blinked a red light every few seconds.

1 **Did he hell!** *(ugs.)* – *Nie im Leben!*
2 **condo(minium)** *(AE)* – *Eigentumswohnung*
3 **opposite** – *gegenüber*

Everything was in place. He was not using matches or petrol or anything which could be detected.

He was being smart.

He had cut the electric wires in the plug of the computer. Placed the waste-paper bin next to it. Then above the bin a **stack**[1] of old boxes containing **ink cartridges**[2].

It would be the perfect accident.

He looked at his watch; it was time.

He walked over to the wire, **knelt down**[3] and took his lighter out. As long as he only burnt the wire, it would look like that was where it started.

He lit the lighter, a delicate yellow flame appearing above it. Then, slowly and carefully, he held it to the wire.

After a second there was a pop and a bang as the wire tore. It was on fire, the flame small but steady, licking at the waste-paper basket then quickly growing.

He stood up and clapped his hands, enjoying the sight as the boxes ignited and spread the damage.

Soon the fire alarms would activate, though hopefully not too soon.

There was one problem though: smoke. The fire had not yet spread enough to do much damage, but there was already a lot of smoke.

The window.

If he opened the window, the smoke would disappear, and the fire would still spread before the alarm went off.

He ran to the window, pushed it open and coughed as the smoke was sucked into the night.

"Yes," he said quietly. "It's working!"

That, however, was when he saw him.

1 **stack** - *Stapel*
2 **ink cartridge** - *Tintenpatrone*
3 **to kneel down** - *sich hinknien*

Standing at a window in the block of flats opposite was an old man.

For a moment Gavin froze as the old man looked directly at his face.

For a moment the old man froze too.

Then, his head coming up and his voice loud enough for everyone to hear, he shouted a single word.

"Fire!"

Gavin watched as the man took a mobile phone from his pocket and began to dial.

Smoke was everywhere now, but knowing he had to escape, Gavin ran to the door and half fell down the stairs until he reached the car park.

Inside the office the fire alarm finally began to ring, the sound causing him to panic even more.

"He saw me!" he said to himself. "He saw my face!"

God! It was all ruined. The old man would identify him to the police. They would know that it was an insurance job.

Unless…

And a dark and **troubling**[1] idea came to his mind.

The old man would not have described him on the telephone. He would wait and tell the police later.

But what, he thought, if there was no later?

Slowly he turned, the idea still forming in his mind, but by the time he reached the entrance to the apartments he knew what he was going to do.

And he knew he must be quick.

He looked up.

It was the second apartment on the third floor.

He opened the door to the building quickly, keeping his face hidden in case there were cameras. Then he ran to the stairs and sped up them, panic, fear and desperation moving him forwards.

1 **troubling** - *beunruhigend*

When he reached the third floor corridor, he checked that no one was there. Seeing that it was empty, he moved to the second door and stopped.

You can do this, Gavin.

Think of the money.

He raised his hand and knocked. "Fire department, open the door, sir," he said, not raising his voice too loudly.

After a few seconds the door opened and the old man smiled at him. "That was very quick, I only..." he started to say, but Gavin moved forwards, covered the man's mouth with his hand and shut the door.

For a second the old man was too surprised to **resist**[1], but then, as he began to struggle to escape, he kicked out, his knee hitting Gavin in the **groin**[2] so that he screamed and fell to the floor. The old man moved backwards, his hands against the walls. "What are you doing?" he shouted. "Help me! Somebody help me."

Gavin was in pain, but he was also angry now. In the distance he could hear fire engines moving in their direction, but they would not be here before he had finished.

"You're dead, old man," he said, watching as his victim retreated.

"No, stay away, I'm warning you!"

Gavin laughed. "Or what?"

The old man's right hand moved to the handle of another door which he pulled open. "Get him Maple! Kill!"

The thing that sped towards Gavin was so fast that he did not know what it was as first.

But when the teeth **ripped**[3] into his throat, he knew.

1 **to resist** - *Widerstand leisten*
2 **groin** - *Leiste*
3 **to rip into sth.** - *etw. zerreißen*

For a few seconds the dog **tore into his flesh**[1], but then finally the old man shouted for it to stop.

Gavin felt blood pumping from the wound, and he suddenly felt too tired to move.

"Why?" asked the old man

"You… saw me… you saw my face… saw me light the fire," Gavin said, knowing that it did not matter anymore.

"Saw you?" the old man said, breaking into a laugh, a sound horrible to Gavin's ears. "Ha! You idiot, I haven't seen a damned thing for nearly twenty years! I'm blind!"

Gavin was beginning to choke on his own blood, but he forced the words from his mouth. "Liar! You saw! You shouted fire!"

The old man laughed again, and his guide dog began to lick at the blood on the floor. "I've got a nose haven't I? I smelt the smoke. And you know what they say: there's no smoke without fire."

1 **to tear into sth.** - *sich über etw. hermachen*

Ottawa, Kanada

Ottawa, die Bundeshauptstadt Kanadas, wurde im frühen 18. Jahrhundert als „Bytown" gegründet. Der Name ‚Ottawa', den die Stadt 1855 erhielt, leitet sich aus der Eigenbenennung eines Urvolkes der Region ab, das aus dem Gebiet der Großen Seen stammte.

Die Stadt zeichnet sich durch ihren sehr hohen Lebensstandard und eine niedrige Arbeitslosenrate aus, die nur geringfügig von der letzten Weltwirtschaftskrise betroffen wurde. Englisch ist mit über 62% Anteil die meistgesprochene Sprache. Knapp 15% sind französischsprachig. In beiden Sprachgruppen ist Zweisprachigkeit auf muttersprachlichem Niveau eher die Ausnahme, und in der englischen Sprachgruppe ist die größte Mehrheit nur einsprachig. Diese Verhältnisse spiegeln sich in den nationalen Statistiken wider: Bundesweit sind Englisch und Französisch die Muttersprachen von ca. 57% bzw. knapp über 21% der Bevölkerung.

26. LITTLE WHITE LIES

"Tell me, was any of it true?" the woman asked, a single tear rolling from her sea-blue eyes.

The second interval was over now, and the lights in the great hall slowly faded to black.

"Would you believe me if I said yes?" the man in the suit next to her asked, his eyes never leaving her face.

A solitary female singer walked onto the stage and began to sing beneath a soft white light.

In the darkness no one could see the couple sitting alone in the private **box**[1] above the stage, but if they could, they would **doubtless**[2] have mistaken the woman's sadness for nothing more than empathy for the tragedy on the stage.

"No," said the woman, a touch of anger replacing the sadness.

"And I don't **blame**[3] you," said the man. "Yet it was almost all true. Ever since the first day we met, I have been honest with you about my feelings, if not about my **true self**[4]."

The woman shook her head, and she felt her cheeks growing warm. "Lies, it was all lies," she hissed.

For a moment the man was silent, and the singer's voice **washed over**[5] them. "Perhaps, but they were **white lies**[6]. Everyone tells white lies. This woman on the stage is pretending to be something she is not. Why can't I?"

1 **box** - *Loge*
2 **doubtless** - *sicherlich*
3 **to blame sb. for sth.** - *jdm. etw. verübeln*
4 **one's true self** - *jds. wahres Ich*
5 **to wash over sb.** - *jdn. überschwemmen*
6 **white lie** - *Notlüge*

She turned to him, her eyes flashing cold with anger. "That's her profession!"

The man nodded. "And this is mine."

For the first time the woman looked down at the gun that he held to her side. "And does your job mean that you're going to kill me?"

For a moment the man looked like she had **struck**[1] him, but then he lowered the gun and put it on the vacant chair to his right. "I would rather die than hurt you. Catherine…"

"**Don't you dare**[2] call me that! Not now!"

He smiled sadly. "Lady North, I never thought that I would **fall for you**[3] like this, but I have. It was never my intention."

"Then what was your intention, Mr Stone, or whatever your real name is?"

"My name is Mark, just like I told you. Stone is just a cover. One of many. And my intention? Well, this was my intention: for you to invite me to share this box with you tonight."

"Why? What are you going to do?"

Mark sighed. "My job, like I told you. My job meant that I had to be here tonight. I learnt about you several months ago. I discovered that you reserve this box every time Medea plays at the Albert Hall. Why is that? Is it because it was the last opera you saw before your parents…"

"Say another word about my family, and I'll scream," Lady Stone hissed.

On the stage the **female lead**[4] had been joined by a tenor, and his deep tones added a sense of **dread**[5] to the hall.

"Forgive me. I should leave you now," Mark said, and for the first time the woman turned to look at his face. The face that she

1 **to strike sb.** - *jdn. schlagen*
2 **Don't you dare!** - *Wage es nicht!*
3 **to fall for sb.** - *jdm. verfallen*
4 **female lead** - *weibliche Hauptrolle*
5 **dread** - *Grauen, Furcht*

had come[1] to love over the past seven weeks. The green eyes that she had stared into for hours each night; the dark hair that she had run her fingers through a hundred times.

"Leave? Why should I let you? You say you won't hurt me, so why shouldn't I shout for help? You're a criminal. I could call the police."

"Perhaps, but I don't think you should. It's true that I do things that are… outside of the law, but sometimes people have to. The man in the next box is an **ambassador**[2] from a country where wars have killed thousands of people."

"So? You intend to kill him for that? He's an ambassador. He makes no decisions for his country: he only represents it."

Mark shook his head. "No, that's not why I intend to kill him. I intend to kill him because of the three young women that he kidnapped and killed the last time he visited one of his neighbouring countries. Everybody knew that it was him, but as an ambassador he was protected, and the threat of war meant that not even the **authorities**[3] dared **bring him to justice**[4]. I work for people who need assistance with this type of thing, but I only ever work for people who are in the right."

Lady North watched him carefully for a moment. "Why should I believe you?"

He shook his head again. "Maybe you shouldn't. I'm sorry, but I have to go now. Catherine…"

"No. Just go."

He stood up. "Tell me, before I do. How did you discover I was not who I said I was?"

She turned back to the opera and silently let the tears fall once more. "Did you really think that I would not check? I'm the sole heir to my family's fortune. I received the email from

1 **to come to do sth.** – *dazu kommen, etw. zu tun*
2 **ambassador** – *Botschafter*
3 **authority** – *Behörde*
4 **to bring sb. to justice** – *jdn. vor Gericht bringen*

my private detective during the interval. You're not the first man to lie to me for his own gain."

"You know that's not why I lied," he said in the darkness.

"Do I? Just go! Take your gun with you."

"Why? There were never any bullets in it. I told you. **I would rather**[1] die than hurt you. I…"

"No," she said, stopping him before the words could leave his lips.

She focused on the stage and on the increasingly strong voices of the singers as the crescendo began to rise. The violins of the orchestra seemed to mirror the pain and anguish she felt within her own heart.

Behind her she heard the curtain to the box move, and she knew that he had left her.

Tears ran down her face more quickly now; her heart seemed to beat in time with the rhythm of the opera, and her chest rose and fell as she fought to calm her breathing.

She knew that she should call for help. Call for somebody to stop him. But she could not.

And then she heard it: the sound of **muffled**[2] voices in the next box. The sound of *his* polite voice offering to refresh their champagne glasses.

As the crescendo rose to its peak, she heard a dull **thud**[3] like someone falling to the floor, and then a scream quickly cut off before it could be heard by the audience in the hall. Then there were more sounds of a **struggle**[4], and she felt fear replacing her anger and misery. The thought of him being hurt was too much for her to bear, but she was frozen with fear.

She was about to stand and run to the other box when she heard the curtain open, and she turned to see him standing

1 **I would rather…** - *Ich würde lieber…*
2 **muffled** - *gedämpft*
3 **thud** - *dumpfer Schlag*
4 **struggle** - *Kampf*

there, his hand pressed to a bloody wound on his shoulder. "Catherine, I know that you'll never believe me now, but I love you," he said, his face pale.

Then there were raised voices in the corridor outside, and he turned and ran.

But I do believe him, she thought suddenly, the realisation freeing her from her fear.

I believe him... and I love him too.

She stood up as she heard feet running in the corridor. Then, without thinking, she picked up the gun that he had left, kicked off her high-heeled shoes and pushed past the curtain. To her left she could see two men moving in the direction of the emergency exit, their hands reaching for the hidden guns under their jackets.

She did not know exactly what she intended to do, but she did not have time to think. She raced after them, the pistol in her hand, and the sound of the opera in her ears. When she pushed open the door to the empty back stairs, she heard someone shouting in front of her and stopped. When she looked up, though, she saw that the two men were not looking at her but at Mark, who had fallen to the floor and was moving silently away from his attackers.

"You killed the ambassador!" the first man shouted.

"Yeah, that's true. It was about time somebody did."

The attacker **swore**[1], kicked Mark in the side then said something to the second man who began to move his hand towards the gun under his jacket.

"Stop!" Lady North heard herself say, the pistol in her hand rising to point at the two men. "Stop, or I will shoot."

On the ground she saw the **defiant**[2] look in Mark's eyes suddenly fill with fear. "Catherine..." he began.

1 **to swear** - *fluchen*
2 **defiant** - *unnachgiebig*

"You shut up too. You've got a lot of apologising to do, and I don't intend on letting these two stop you."

The two men watched her silently. "You won't shoot," the first one said.

"Really?" she asked, pulling back the **hammer of the pistol**[1]. "Are you that sure? I'm not a very good shot, but from this distance I'm going to hit one of you before you can get me," she hissed, her sea-blue eyes blazing fiercely.

For a moment none of them spoke, and there was only the sound of the opera to fill the tense silence.

Then, from inside, there was a scream, and it was obvious that the ambassador's body had been found.

"We're going now," she said to Mark. "Get up and start moving."

Mark nodded and with an effort forced himself to stand. Slowly, the gun never leaving the two men, she walked to him and put his arm over her shoulder. Then, with a final glance at the two men, she began to help him down the stairwell.

Only when they had reached the bottom of the stairs and pushed open the fire escape door did she throw the gun to the floor.

"We need to get to my car," she said, helping him to run.

"Catherine, the gun: there were no bullets in it. You did know that?" he said as they struggled to get away, the Royal Albert Hall ablaze with light behind them.

"I knew that. So?"

"So you lied" he said with a weak **grin**[2].

"A white lie," she said, allowing herself to smile too. "Just a little white lie."

1 **hammer of the pistol** - *Hahn der Pistole*
2 **grin** - *Grinsen*

Die **Royal Albert Hall**, von Königin Viktoria 1871 eröffnet und nach ihrem verstorbenen Königsgemahl Prinz Albert benannt, ist eine Veranstaltungshalle, die bis zu 9500 Besucher fasst. Sie ist als Wohlfahrtsorganisation eingetragen und erhält keine Gelder vom Staat.

Die Halle ist bekannt für ihre klassischen Musikveranstaltungen wie die Konzertreihe „The BBC Proms" und Opernaufführungen. Hier finden jedoch auch Veranstaltungen anderer Art statt: Seit ihrer Gründung 1997 wird hier jährlich die ATP Champions Tour abgeschlossen. Darüber hinaus öffnet die Halle ihre Türen für Filmpremieren und Popmusik-Konzerte. Eric Clapton hat in dieser Halle schon fast 200-mal ein Konzert gegeben.

27. WHAT DOES NOT KILL YOU

A light rain was falling as the police car slowly made its way along the quiet country roads, grey clouds sitting above the Whangamarino wetlands in a way that suggested they would never leave.

Constable[1] Cline watched the green landscape of forests, **swamps**[2] and **peat bogs**[3] in silence, the question forming in her mind but not quite reaching her lips.

"Go on," Detective Cole said, his hands on the **steering wheel**[4] and his eyes on the road, "ask me. You know you want to."

Cline looked at him. His face was serious as always, his grey eyes as unreadable as the clouds above them. He was not a man without humour, but he was also not a man to waste his words. "Okay," she said. "Do you really think he's dead?"

"Does it matter what I think? The **inquest**[5] has agreed to declare him dead. So he's dead."

Cline looked back at the swamps and the miles of endless wilderness. "So why are you coming out here? You don't have to. You could have sent someone else. You could have sent me."

Cline was a plain woman with intelligent brown eyes and a sincere face. The police uniform that she wore **suited**[6] her, though she **looked forward**[7] to the day she would be made a detective and could wear a smart suit like Cole.

1 **constable** - *Polizist*
2 **swamp** - *Sumpf*
3 **peat bog** - *Torfmoor*
4 **steering wheel** - *Lenkrad*
5 **inquest** - *Untersuchungsausschuss*
6 **to suit sb.** - *jdm. gut stehen (Kleidung)*
7 **to look forward to sth.** - *sich auf etw. freuen*

"Why do you think I'm here?" Cole asked as a wooden house by the side of a forest appeared in front of them.

She thought for a moment. "Because you want to look her in the face when you tell her."

"Maybe you're right," he said, slowing the car as they entered the **driveway**[1] of the isolated property.

"I am right." She had learned over the past months of working with the detective that the only way to talk to him was in the same direct way that he talked to you. "What I don't understand is why."

Cole stopped the car. The gardens around the house were wild but beautiful. Long **reeds**[2] rose up out of the ponds, and plants grew along the thin paths that led to the forests and the swamps.

"You saw the reports. You should know exactly why I want to see her face."

"You think she killed him."

"Why not? Thirty per cent of all murders are committed by family members. Mr Harris had no family apart from her."

They got out of the car, and Cline adjusted her uniform, a slight feeling of **anxiety**[3] reaching her stomach. "What should I say? I've never..."

"You've never told a **next of kin**[4] that their loved one is dead. Well, you don't have to say anything. Consider this a lesson, but I doubt it will be the most typical of **encounters**[5]," Cole said, pulling the collar of his jacket up against the rain.

As they walked towards the wooden steps that led to the porch of the house, Cline saw a woman standing at the window. She was about fifty, perhaps, with **auburn**[6] hair tied up in a

1 **driveway** - *Einfahrt*
2 **reed** - *Schilf*
3 **anxiety** - *Unbehagen*
4 **next of kin** - *nächster Angehöriger*
5 **encounter** - *Begegnung*
6 **auburn** - *rostrot*

severe knot on her head and her face **devoid**[1] of make-up or hospitality.

Before they reached the top step, the door opened, and Mrs Harris spoke. "I know what you've come to say, Detective, but you're wrong." And with that she turned and walked into the house leaving the door open for them to follow.

It was a simple but charming place. A fire in the corner of the room was burning gently, and there were paintings of the wetlands decorating the walls. To their right the door to the kitchen was open, and a delicious smell of **stew**[2] or soup filled the entire house.

"Mrs Harris, this is Constable Cline."

The older woman looked at Cline for a second then seemed to **dismiss**[3] her from her thoughts. "I suppose I should offer you a drink. Tea?"

"No, thank you, we're fine. Perhaps we could sit."

Mrs Harris nodded to the sofa then took an armchair opposite them and waited. "Well, say it then."

"Mrs Harris, the coroner is prepared to declare your husband dead. He's been missing now for seven months, and the conclusion made by the inquest is that he has suffered an accidental death somewhere within the wetlands. This decision allows you to **claim**[4] his life insurance."

Silence filled the room, and Cline felt her eyes unable to move from Mrs Harris' face. Maybe she had been attractive once, but if so, it was gone now, replaced by an ugly coldness. "No, he's not dead. I know that he's not. So I don't want that money."

Cline glanced at Cole, but his expression was impossible to read. Had he expected something else? Was he waiting for

1 **to be devoid of sth.** - *an etw. mangeln*
2 **stew** - *Eintopf*
3 **to dismiss sth./sb. from one's thoughts** - *etw./jdn. ausblenden*
4 **to claim a life insurance** - *Anprüche aus einer Lebensversicherung geltend machen*

something that would show she had killed her husband for the money?

"You're so sure?" the detective asked.

"I am."

"And tell me, Mrs Harris, if, as you believe, your husband is alive, would that make you happy?"

For the first time an expression other than **impatience**[1] appeared on Mrs Harris' face, yet it was not the anger that Cline had expected: it was a smile.

"My husband is alive, Detective, and yes, that does make me happy."

Cole shook his head. "See, that's what I've never been able to believe. Mrs Cole, the first time we met, a week after your husband's disappearance, you had a **bruise**[2] on your face and a cut on your lip. They were not new **injuries**[3]: they were maybe two weeks old. You said that you had fallen down the steps in front of your house, yet I knew that you were lying. I've seen enough **domestic-abuse**[4] cases to know that your husband was **beating**[5] you."

The smile did not move from Mrs Harris' face. "Detective, what would you know about married life? There's no ring on your finger, nor on hers," she said with a nod of the head to Cline. "You think my husband **abused**[6] me? He did not. Did he sometimes have to teach me lessons? Yes, he did."

"Lessons?" Cline asked before she could stop herself.

Mrs Harris' eyes turned to look at her. "Yes, lessons. In spite of all your modern city teaching, you have no idea how a real marriage works. My husband taught me more than anyone. When I made a mistake, he would teach me the right way to do something. Did it hurt sometimes? Yes. But like he always said,

1 **impatience** - *Ungeduld*
2 **bruise** - *Bluterguss*
3 **injury** - *Verletzung*
4 **domestic abuse** - *häusliche Gewalt*
5 **to beat** - *schlagen*
6 **to abuse sb.** - *jdn. misshandeln*

what doesn't kill you makes you stronger. And I'm strong now, oh yes, very strong."

Cline looked away, shocked by the revelation.

"Fine," Cole said. "So you let him beat you for your mistakes. And what about his mistakes? What about Lisa Pool?"

Mrs Harris stood up suddenly, her eyes **blazing**[1] with anger. "**How dare you**[2]? Get out! Go on, get out of my house!"

Cole stood too. "He was having an affair with her. She was the one who let us know that he was missing. Why was that, Mrs Harris? Why did you never call the police? Your husband goes out duck hunting in the swamps one day and doesn't come back. Did you not call because you thought he was with her, or because you knew exactly where he was… and didn't want anyone to know?"

Mrs Harris looked from Cole to Cline then shook her head, the anger disappearing as quickly as it came. "Idiots. You're all idiots. You'll never understand. Now get out!"

Cole nodded, and Cline led the way to the door, pushing it open and stepping back into the light rain.

As they walked back to the car, she could feel a pair of eyes on the back of her neck. "So?" she asked. "What do you think?"

"The same thing I've always thought. There's a **capacity**[3] for violence in that woman. I can feel it." He looked up at the window where Mrs Harris stood. "The thing is, Mr Harris and his abuse is probably what gave her that capacity. Maybe I should just let this one go."

Cline shook her head. "You know, maybe there's another possibility. Maybe he's not dead. Maybe they faked the whole thing together for the life insurance money."

The rain began to fall harder, and as Mrs Harris moved away from the window, Cole shook his head. "No, he's dead. I can feel it in my bones."

1 **to blaze** – *funkeln*
2 **How dare you?** – *Wie können Sie es wagen?*
3 **capacity** – *Potential*

Inside the house Mrs Harris listened as the police drove away then she went to the kitchen and filled a bowl with steaming hot stew. Then, taking an umbrella from near the back door of the house, she stepped out into the rain and walked slowly down the wild path that cut through the forest.

When she reached a small clearing about three miles from the house, she stopped and put the bowl down on the wet, muddy ground.

"It was the police," she said. "That Detective Cole. He's a bad one, he is. He doesn't understand anything." She picked up a large stick that was leaning against a tree. "Anyway, they've gone now. They came to tell me that I can claim the insurance money." She shook her head. "And he talked about… her."

Mrs Harris moved to the middle of the clearing where there was a small peat bog. In the centre of the bog, a large piece of wood was covering something. She used the stick to move it then she smiled.

"Well, anyway, here's your dinner."

She used the stick to push the bowl out to the middle of the bog. There, with pale skin, the fat completely gone from the face; was Mr Harris' head.

As she pushed the food closer, his eyes slowly opened, and his lips moved.

"How you fell into this old bog I don't know," said Mrs Harris kindly. "I guess it was God's punishment for what you did with that woman. You were just lucky that I found you."

Mr Harris' lips moved again, the eyes pleading.

"What? Kill you? Oh no. I would never do that. Remember dear, it's just like you always say, *what doesn't kill you makes you stronger*."

Whangamarino Sumpfgebiet, Neuseeland

Das **Whangamarino-Sumpfgebiet**, das sich im Nordwesten der Nordinsel Neuseelands befindet, ist eine der wichtigsten Regionen dieser Art im Land. Es erstreckt sich über eine Fläche von ca. 72 km^2 und besteht aus Sümpfen, Torfmooren, Flüssen und Wäldern. Viele seltene oder gar nur dort vorkommende Pflanzenarten und der Artenreichtum an Wasser- und Sumpfvögeln und Fischarten bieten für viele Biologen und Vogelkundler ein spannendes Forschungsfeld. Etwa ein Zehntel des Sumpfgebiets befindet sich im Besitz der „Fish and Game New Zealand", einer Ratsvereinigung von Jägern und Sportanglern, die sich landesweit nicht nur um die Interessen der Jäger und Angler, sondern auch um den Erhalt und die Ausweitung der Artenvielfalt kümmert.

28. A SKELETON IN THE CLOSET

In New York **housemates**[1] are never hard to find. You put an **ad**[2] online, place a few posters at the library, the local gym, a friendly **corner shop**[3].

By the time you get back to your apartment, the red light on your answering machine is blinking. You hit play, and you try to take notes from the mix of different accents and voices that are all trying to convince you that they are **the one**[4]. That they are the person who should enter your home. The person who will be living just **yards**[5] away from where you sleep at night.

After that you have two or three weeks of interviews: an opportunity to separate the **vaguely**[6] normal candidates from the crazies who seem to populate the Big Apple.

Just look up the next time you are walking down the street. Look up at all of those apartment buildings rising into the sky. Think about all of the strange people living together like rabbits. Most of them complete strangers once. Now they share a door, a space, an address, and all just because of that first ad.

That was not, however, the way that I met Suki.

It was a rainy Sunday afternoon. I remember because my hair was **soaked**[7] by the time I reached the coffee house on the corner. Jack was already there, with a grin on his face and a comment about my appearance.

1 **housemate** - *Mitbewohner(in)*
2 **ad** - *Anzeige*
3 **corner shop** - *Tante-Emma-Laden*
4 **to be the one** - *der/die Richtige sein*
5 **yard** - *Yard (0,914 Meter)*
6 **vaguely** - *annähernd*
7 **soaked** - *pitschnass*

I remember thanking him sarcastically, and he replied *that is what friends are for.*

Friends. Yes, Jack and I were friends.

Had there been a time when I wanted more than that?

Yes.

However, that is not important. I knew that I was not the kind of girl that Jack would ever be interested in. He liked educated, artistic women **whereas**[1] I was just his stupid friend Maggie.

But anyway, like I said, that is not important. This is not a story about Jack and me. It is about Suki, the woman who I would meet in that warm, quiet coffee house.

"So?" Jack asked. "When are you going to advertise for a new housemate? When did Cathy move out? Two months ago? You could save a lot of money if you found someone."

I put the large cappuccino down and shook my head. "I just can't do it. I hate looking for housemates. I hate letting those strangers into my apartment."

"Cathy was okay," Jack grinned.

"You mean she was hot. She was not okay. She was **filthy**[2]: she never cleaned."

"Yeah, but she had a great figure."

I shook my head.

"Excuse me."

The polite voice that interrupted my thoughts belonged to an Asian lady. She was sitting on the table next to ours, and I could not remember seeing her before that moment.

She apologised for listening to our conversation then mentioned that she was looking for somewhere to live herself.

We spoke for some time. She was dressed neatly in **subtle**[3] colours, and her short black hair was perfectly combed. At one

1 **whereas** - *während*
2 **filthy** - *dreckig*
3 **subtle** - *dezent*

point I recall seeing the way that Jack was looking into her eyes, and a part of me **felt a stab of jealousy**[1].

Despite this moment of doubt, I knew that she was going to be my new housemate.

She moved into the apartment the next Friday evening. I was there with a bottle of champagne to greet her, yet when she arrived she explained that she was up very early the next day, so I let her unpack her things alone. When I saw her on Saturday evening, I asked her if she wanted to go to the coffee shop.

"I'm sorry, Maggie, but I have to work again tomorrow. I work a lot, to be honest: the art gallery is very busy at the moment. I'm afraid we may not see much of each other."

On Monday I went back to work, and for the next few days I almost forgot that I had a new housemate.

"So when are we going to go out for drinks?" Jack asked on the phone one night.

"I don't know. I never see her."

The sensation of living with someone but never seeing them is a very odd sensation **indeed**[2].

It is like living with a ghost.

I **would hear**[3] the sounds of the shower in the morning. I would hear her gentle footsteps in the hall and the sound of the front door opening and closing in the middle of the night. Sometimes I thought that I heard voices in her room.

A man's voice?

A familiar man's voice?

Once I even **awoke**[4] in the middle of the night and thought that I heard Suki shouting a name, though perhaps that was just a dream.

1 **to feel a stab of jealousy** – *einen Anflug von Eifersucht verspüren*
2 **indeed** – *durchaus*
3 **I would hear...** – *Ich hörte immer ...*
4 **to awake** – *aufwachen*

It continued like this for five weeks. Suki, my perfect housemate, was a ghost to me now.

Until the night that I saw the **body**[1].

It was nearly two in the morning, yet I was awake in my bedroom, a book in my hands and sleep impossible due to the strong coffee that I had drunk earlier that night with Jack.

When I heard the sound of the front door opening, I turned the light off quickly, although I was not exactly sure why.

My bedroom door was open slightly, no more than a **crack**[2], so when I saw her slowly pass my door, I knew that she could not know that I was sitting there watching in the dark.

And that was when I saw it. She moved slowly past the door, walking backwards, and in her hands she dragged a large black bag. A large black bag with what I can only say looked like bones sticking out of the top.

"It was a body, Jack!" I hissed down the phone at him early the next morning.

"Maggie, you don't know that. You must **be mistaken**[3]. You've not been yourself these last few weeks."

"That's because of her! Jack, you have to believe me... I..." I stopped talking and listened. I was in the bathroom, a knife in my hand and the door locked. In the hallway I could hear her steps and waited until I heard the front door open and close. "She's gone out. Where are you?"

"I'm nearly at your building."

"Okay, listen. When you get here, wait at the **lobby**[4]. I have to see what's in her room. If you see her coming back, call me."

"Wait, Maggie, I don't even know what she looks like."

"Of course you do!"

"No, Maggie, I..." he started to say, but I hung up.

1 **body** - *Leiche*
2 **crack** - *Spalt*
3 **to be mistaken** - *sich irren*
4 **lobby** - *Eingangshalle*

It had to be now.

I opened the bathroom door slowly and looked around. The apartment was silent and empty. With the knife still in my hand, I walked to the closed door of Suki's room.

"Suki?" I asked quietly.

There was no reply. I put my hand on the door and pushed.

Inside, the curtains were half drawn, the light from the window dancing around the room.

Around me a perfectly normal room.

There were pictures of her family on a table by the bed, shoes in a **neat**[1] row near the window, a collection of books on the shelf.

Could I have made a mistake?

I moved to the **closet**[2] in the corner of the room, and for a moment I hesitated before I opened it.

And there it was.

The black bag was hanging up like a dress. Inside it I could see the same bright-white bones that I had seen the night before.

"Maggie."

I screamed as I turned. She was standing right behind me.

"Suki, what is this?" I asked, my voice shrill with terror.

She looked at me with her mysterious eyes. "Maggie, this is very wrong. You aren't allowed to enter my room." She moved towards me, and I stepped back, the knife behind me. "This is a skeleton, Maggie, from the art gallery. I use it for my drawings." She opened the bag further and revealed where the bones were held together by metal.

"Oh God," I said, feeling like an idiot. "I'm so sorry."

Suki just looked at me. "I think you should go now, Maggie."

I nodded and quickly left her room, closing the door behind me.

It was then that I felt the hand on my shoulder, and I turned quickly, the knife rising defensively.

1 **neat** - *ordentlich*
2 **closet** *(AE)* - *Kleiderschrank*

"Maggie!" Jack shouted as he stepped back.

"Jack, I'm sorry."

"What are you doing with a knife, Maggie?" he asked, his face worried.

"I was scared, but it's okay, you were right: I made a mistake. It was just a skeleton for her drawings," I said. "But…" I thought for a second, "why didn't you call me when you saw her coming back?"

"She's here? Maggie, I tried to tell you, I don't know what she looks like."

"Of course you do! You met her that day in the coffee shop."

"What? Maggie, are you okay? I've never met her. I've just heard you talk about her constantly for the last five weeks."

"What..?" I heard myself ask, but Jack was already pushing open the door to Suki's room.

"Maggie? I don't understand."

I followed him into the room.

The empty room.

There were no pictures, no shoes, no books.

I moved to the mirror and stopped.

And then I began to understand.

I looked into the mirror.

"Suki," I whispered, and in the reflection I saw her smile. She lifted a hand to her short black hair, and I saw the knife that she was holding.

That I was holding.

That we were holding.

Jack had never wanted me. He had always wanted an educated, artistic woman.

Well, now he could have Suki.

"Look in the closet, Jack," we said.

When he turned, we lifted the knife and moved behind him.

So, in the end Suki was the perfect housemate. So perfect that Jack never left us after that.

So perfect that he never will.

"Give me your tired, your poor,
Your huddled[1] masses yearning to breathe free,
The wretched[2] refuse of your teeming[3] shore.
Send these, the homeless, tempest-tossed[4], to me:
I lift my lamp beside the golden door."

Diese Worte stammen aus dem Sonett „The New Colossus" aus dem Jahr 1883 von Emma Lazarus und sind in eine Tafel eingraviert, die ursprünglich am Podest der Freiheitsstatue in **New York City** angebracht war, inzwischen jedoch im Statue of Liberty Museum ausgestellt ist. Vor der Ära der Flugreisen zogen die Menschen, die aus anderen Kontinenten in New York eintrafen, auf Schiffen an der „Lady Liberty" vorbei.

New York ist heute eine der größten Metropolen der Vereinigten Staaten und eine der am dichtesten bevölkerten Regionen der Welt. Aufgrund der Vielfalt der Kulturen ist es auch die sprachenreichste Stadt der Welt: Man schätzt, dass in den insgesamt 280 Wohnvierteln der Stadt ca. 800 verschiedene Sprachen gesprochen werden.

1 **huddled** – *geknechtet*
2 **wretched** – *armselig*
3 **teeming** – *gedrängt*
4 **tempest-tossed** – *vom Sturm getrieben*

29. TO DIE FOR

"Look at this place. It's a palace," Detective Loux said, removing his hat and looking up at the elaborately-painted ceiling of the hotel's lobby. The reception was beneath a vast **domed**[1] roof, the type of which you would expect to find in a cathedral, not in a holiday resort. And the entire space was filled with palm trees, exotic flowers, statues of South Africa's wildlife and patiently-smiling attendants, who were ready to supply the guests with anything they might desire.

"What? You've never been here?" asked Detective Smit, opening his white shirt so that he could enjoy the cool breeze of the air conditioning.

"Of course not," Loux said with a shake of his head. "I've only ever seen it from the outside."

Smit laughed and slapped his partner on the back. "Well, **you're in for a treat**[2]. I say we **get** this thing **wrapped up**[3] quickly and get some drinks by the pool. You need to **familiarise**[4] yourself with the place. That's what a good cop would do."

Loux shook his head but smiled as they walked over to the long mahogany reception desk.

The two detectives were as opposite as it was possible to be. Loux was tall, with dark skin and **jet-black**[5] hair, while Smit

1 **domed** - *gewölbt*
2 **You're in for a treat.** - *Du kannst dich auf etwas ganz Besonderes freuen.*
3 **to get sth. wrapped up** - *etw. eingetütet bekommen (zum Abschluss bringen)*
4 **to familiarise oneself with sth.** - *sich mit etw. vertraut machen*
5 **jet-black** - *samtschwarz*

was short and fair, with a grin that **mocked**[1] his partner's more serious **demeanour**[2].

"Wrap it up quickly? You heard what the chief said. This doesn't sound like it's going to be quick."

"Yeah well," Smit said, placing a stick of gum in his mouth and beginning to chew. "The chief must have made a mistake. I **bet**[3] we'll be at the side of the pool by five."

They reached the reception desk, **flashed**[4] their badges and were told the room number.

"They could at least show us the way," Smit said as they **headed towards**[5] one of the lifts. "I don't even know if this is..."

The door to the lift opened, and a hotel maid in a blue uniform stepped out, a pile of towels in her hands and a smile on her mouth.

"Hello," said Smit. "Say, is this the right elevator for room 732?"

The maid looked at him with a pair of big blue eyes that Smit thought he might drown in. "No, sorry, it's the opposite tower. You need the lift over there."

Smit thanked her and watched her walk away while shaking his head. "You see that? Even the staff are **gorgeous**[6]. She had eyes to die for."

"Yeah sure, come on," Loux said, heading for the opposite lift.

As they reached the seventh floor, they could smell the smoke. "I hate crimes that involve fire," said Smit, taking his gum out and sticking it onto the wall. "You know why? Because I hate Marks. He's always so serious. You remember that

1 **to mock sth.** - *etw. verspotten*
2 **demeanour** - *Auftreten*
3 **to bet** - *wetten*
4 **to flash sth.** - *etw. aufblitzen lassen*
5 **to head towards sth.** - *sich auf etw. zubewegen*
6 **gorgeous** - *umwerfend*

arson[1] case back in Rustenburg? He started shouting at me for something... I can't remember what."

Loux shook his head as they walked along the corridor. "You started smoking."

"So?"

"So the place was still covered in petrol."

Smit laughed. "Oh yeah. Ah well, **good job I've quit**[2]."

They reached the room. Two cops in uniform were standing outside, their faces looking unhappy. "Hey boys, what's up?" asked Smit.

"It's not nice in there, Detective," Constable Jones said.

"Ah, nothing we haven't seen before."

"I bet you've never seen this," said the other, his face pale.

"Yeah? What is it?"

Jones shook his head. "We don't really know, sir. The fire alarm went off. When security got here, the door was locked so they used their own keys to get in. There was smoke everywhere and a burning body on the bed. After they **put the fire out**[3], they searched the place, but there was no one else there."

Loux raised an eyebrow. "So? Obviously the murderer left before security got here."

"Well, according to the guest in the opposite room, Mr Cane..."

The door to the opposite room opened. "That's me, I'm Mr Cane," said an elderly Briton with a colonial-style white moustache. "No one left that room! I heard the alarm, and I opened my door. My wife Margery phoned reception. I **did not leave this spot**[4]. I tell you: no one left that room!"

"Okay, thank you, sir. One of the constables will take a formal statement from you in a minute," said Loux with a polite smile.

1 **arson** - *Brandstiftung*
2 **Good job I've quit.** - *Zum Glück habe ich aufgehört.*
3 **to put a fire out** - *ein Feuer löschen*
4 **not to leave a spot** - *sich nicht vom Fleck rühren*

Mr Cane shook his head. "The man was **blind drunk**[1]. He nearly fell into me when I saw him here in the corridor."

"When was that, sir?" asked Loux.

"About an hour before the alarm went off."

"Thank you, that's all for now." The man closed the door.

"What do we need his word for?" asked Smit. "Surely they've got cameras in all the corridors?"

"Yes, sir," said Jones. "But the video just confirms what Mr Cane said. No one came in or out of this room until security got here. They entered the room, extinguished the flames...but they were too late."

Smit shook his head. "Well then, what the hell are we doing here? We're **homicide**[2] detectives. No murderer: no murder. No murder: no us. Come on Loux, let's **hit that bar**[3] early."

The door to room 732 opened, and a serious-faced man in a green plastic suit and white gloves looked at them.

"Marks," said Loux, with a nod of the head.

"Marks," said Smit, with a look of **annoyance**[4].

Marks stared at them coldly, passed them face masks and walked back into the room.

"One of you stay here; one of you come with us," Loux said to the uniformed cops. Neither looked happy, but Jones nodded and followed them into the room.

The scene was horrific.

The ceiling of the room was black. The bed was a blackened mess of burnt sheets and melted mattress, with the **metal springs**[5] visible and pressing into the chargrilled corpse.

"Who is it? Smit asked.

1 **blind drunk** - *stockbetrunken*
2 **homicide** - *Tötung*
3 **to hit the bar** *(ugs.)* - *zur Bar gehen*
4 **annoyance** - *Ärger, Verärgerung*
5 **metal spring** - *Metallfeder*

"Mr Thorpe," the uniformed cop said. "American **expat**[1] who lives in Johannesburg. Married, no kids, a lot of money and a **gambling addiction**[2]. A regular of Sun City."

"The wife?" Loux asked.

"Not here. The girl at reception was pretty useful: she told me all about Mr Thorpe. He comes here three or four times a year. Always alone. Always gambling. He drinks by the pool every afternoon. Sleeps for a few hours in the evening, hits the casino at night. Then, win or lose, he finds a woman to bring back to his room. Normally the type of woman you have to pay for."

"The good life," said Smit, walking to the large windows that opened onto the balcony. "Okay Marks, tell us how he set himself on fire with a cigarette in his sleep so we can get out of here."

"I wish I could," said Marks. "But I've inspected the scene carefully; there's no obvious **incendiary**[3]. No cigarette, no matches, no electronics. More importantly, there was not enough smoke in this room to render him unconscious. The fire only burnt for a few minutes, but it burnt quickly. And from this initial inspection it seems the victim did not even try to extinguish the flames, nor move from the bed. To be honest, Detectives, I don't believe this man died from his **burns**[4]. I believe he died from the shock.

Loux looked at Marks. The man had never failed to give them an answer before, but today he seemed to be hesitating.

"So what? He just exploded into flames, but lay there until his heart failed?" asked Smit.

Jones nodded his head. "It happens. **Spontaneous combustion**[5]."

Smit laughed. "Yeah sure!"

1 **expat** - *im Ausland lebender Mensch*
2 **gambling addiction** - *Spielsucht*
3 **incendiary** - *Brandmittel*
4 **burn** - *Brandwunde*
5 **spontaneous combustion** - *spontane Verbrennung*

Loux looked at Marks. "That's just a myth, right?"

Marks shrugged. "I thought so…but it does look like that."

"That doesn't explain why he didn't move. If I was set on fire I'd dive straight off the balcony into the pool."

Loux shook his head. "The neighbour said Thorpe was blind drunk. What if he was wrong? What if someone had drugged Thorpe? There are chemicals which can paralyse a person, right, Marks?"

Marks shrugged. "Perhaps, but without an incendiary it still doesn't explain the fire."

Smit swore. "Damn it man, this is your job. Find out how he did it so we can go to the bar."

Marks gave him an angry look. "Well, Detective, maybe you could do your job and look for something **flammable**[1]."

Smit and Loux began to search the room, but there was nothing obvious. "What about this?" asked Loux, holding up a bottle of tanning oil.

Marks shook his head. "No, not strong enough."

"Give me that, I need a bit of colour to attract the ladies," said Smit reaching for the bottle, opening it and putting some of the contents onto his hands. "Jesus, not strong enough? This stuff stinks."

Marks looked at him then walked across the room and took the bottle. He poured a little onto his hand and looked across at Loux. "This isn't tanning lotion. It's acetone. A highly-flammable liquid."

"Ah Jesus, it's all over my hands!" said Smit.

"So this is a murder?"

Marks turned back to the body. "Perhaps. If someone changed his tanning oil for this, but..."

"What?"

"Well, it's a very risky way of killing someone."

1 **flammable** - *leichtentzündlich*

"Why? What's risky about that? You just let him rub it on, and then you throw a match at the guy," said Smit, opening a drawer and **wiping his hands**[1] on the dead guy's socks.

"Sure, but there was no one in the room to throw a match. There was nothing here that could have **ignited**[2] the acetone. It's a mystery."

"Hey look, his wallet," said Smit, taking it from the drawer and opening it.

Loux moved to the window and stared out at the hotel balconies and the high South African sun that hung above the hotel. "Unless...Marks, when I was a kid back in Bela-Bela, we sometimes used to use a **magnifying glass**[3] to burn ants. We **would**[4] hold it over them until the sun was so concentrated there was a flame."

Marks walked to the window and looked up at the balconies in the tower opposite where they had already been. "It could work. The **perpetrator**[5] would have to wait for a long time and get the magnification of the light just right. So they'd need access to one of those higher rooms over there. But God, what type of person would do that? First, exchange his tanning oil for acetone then drug him so he lies paralysed on his bed and then ignite him, knowing that even as he burns he is still alive, still conscious. They would have to be a monster."

"Or a wife who's discovered her husband's infidelity!" Smit suddenly said, turning and holding up a picture that he had found in the wallet.

"That's the wife?"

"Yeah, remind you of anyone?" he said, throwing the picture to Loux as he ran to the balcony and desperately searched the crowds of people entering and leaving the lobby.

1 **to wipe one's hands on sth.** - *sich die Hände an etw. abwischen*
2 **to ignite** - *anzünden*
3 **magnifying glass** - *Lupe*
4 **We would...** - *Wir haben immer...*
5 **perpetrator** - *Täter(in)*

Loux looked at the picture and shook his head. "What are you talking about, Smit?"

"The eyes!" his partner shouted. "Look at her eyes!"

Loux stared at the big blue eyes. "What?!"

Smit ran past him and back into the corridor. "Eyes to die for, Loux! She's got eyes to die for!"

Vergnügungskomplex Sun City, Südafrika

→ **Sun City** ist der Name eines Luxushotelresorts in Südafrika nahe der Stadt Rustenburg. Das Resort wurde 1979 eröffnet und befand sich bis zum Ende der Apartheid innerhalb der Homelands von Bophuthatswana. Homelands waren Gebiete, die vom Regime Südafrikas geschaffen wurden und in die die schwarzafrikanische Bevölkerung zwangsumgesiedelt werden sollte; international waren die Homelands nicht anerkannt. Die Vereinten Nationen setzten einen Boykott gegen Südafrika durch, um die Politik der Apartheid zu verurteilen. Ungeachtet dieses Boykotts traten viele berühmte Künstler in Sun City auf. Das veranlasste den Musiker Steven Van Zandt, 1985 das Projekt „Artists United against Apartheid" zu gründen und den Song „Sun City" zu schreiben, in dem sich die Künstler gemeinsam gegen einen Auftritt in Sun City aussprachen.

30. MURDER IN THE DARKNESS

The darkness was cold, consuming and complete; however, the silence was not.

At first, when the lights had failed, there had been **gasps**[1] of panic and muttered reassurances that everything was okay.

As the seconds had become minutes, however, the darkness had filled not only the **carriage**[2] of the train but also the hearts and minds of the passengers, and the voices had faded to almost nothing.

Yet it was not just fear of the darkness that had silenced the voices, although this had undoubtedly contributed to the shared tension. No, it was the thought of where they were. The thought of why that darkness was so cold, consuming and complete.

The thought of the tunnel which surrounded them.

So in the darkness they sat and they waited, and there was still the occasional **hushed**[3] voice saying that the lights would return in just a moment. However, the thoughts of the people in the carriage were all of one thing.

They were thinking about the tunnel.

They were thinking about how deep and dark the tunnel was. They were thinking about the enormous weight of the sea above them.

For this was no ordinary tunnel. It was a thirty-one-mile-long tunnel buried two-hundred-and-fifty **feet**[4] beneath the sea.

It was the Channel Tunnel.

1 **gasp** - *Keuchen*
2 **carriage** - *Wagen*
3 **hushed** - *gedämpft*
4 **foot** - *Fuß (0,3048 Meter)*

And there was a quiet sense of **dread**[1] within the almost empty carriage of the passenger train.

Nick's mind **rewound**[2] an hour or so to the moment where he had boarded the train at St Pancras station. It was a cold February evening, and the air was decorated with a thin fog which had covered the glass ceiling of the terminal.

Taking his seat by the window, he stared at his reflection for a moment, noticing the dark rings under his eyes and running a hand through his chestnut hair to straighten it.

Idly[3], he turned to the few passengers sharing his carriage, inspecting their faces and guessing at their characters to pass the time.

In the far corner there was a thin and elderly woman, a book in her hand and a delicate **lace hat**[4] upon her head. A grandmother journeying to France to see her grandchildren, perhaps? Or a widow returning to the place where she had first met her **late**[5] husband?

On the table opposite the elderly lady, an American couple were talking about their trip to London, commenting on everything from the **quaint**[6] little houses to the high price of a ticket on the Underground.

Nick turned away from them to look at a younger couple on the next table. The man was flicking through[7] a newspaper, and the woman was reading a French phrase book. Occasionally, the woman would let her eyes move from the phrase book to the ring on her left hand. Then she would smile and look up at the man.

1 **dread** - *Grauen, Furcht*
2 **to rewind** - *zurückspulen*
3 **idly** - *träge*
4 **lace hat** - *Hut aus Spitze*
5 **late** - *hier: verstorben*
6 **quaint** - *urig*
7 **to flick through sth.** - *etw. durchblättern*

Nick smiled too. It was easy enough to guess that they were going on their honeymoon.

Behind him he heard two men conversing in an eastern European language that he could not identify. Turning his head, he saw that they were both wearing dark suits and had serious expressions on their tanned faces. For a moment Nick watched them, trying to decide which country they were from. Then one of the men noticed him, and both stopped talking, their eyes focusing on him with an intensity that made him look away.

He was about to take a book from his bag when he noticed a woman in a black leather jacket boarding the train. She looked at her ticket and then spoke in French to the **attendant**[1] who directed her to a seat at the back of the carriage.

For a moment Nick watched her, but then, not wanting to annoy her too, he turned back to his coffee.

On the platform the **conductor**[2] looked at his watch, and then raised his whistle to his lips.

"Wait!" a voice shouted. A slightly overweight man in a white shirt and **smart**[3] black trousers was running to catch the train. His thin blond hair was a mess, and his round face was covered in sweat.

With an expression of annoyance the conductor signalled for him to be quick, and the man jumped onto the train with a small black briefcase in his right hand.

Curious, Nick watched as the man looked back at the platform as if he was expecting to see someone. Then, with a satisfied smile he hit the button on the door to the carriage and entered, breathing hard with sweat **soaking**[4] his white shirt.

As the man began to walk along the **aisle**[5], he turned his head quickly from side to side, noticing the faces of the other

1 **attendant** - *Zugbegleiter*
2 **conductor** - *Schaffner(in)*
3 **smart** - *schick*
4 **to soak** - *durchnässen*
5 **aisle** - *Gang*

passengers. When he saw the two men in dark suits watching him, he stopped for a moment, an expression of fear moving across his face. Then the men turned away, and he continued to move along the aisle until he reached the table opposite Nick's.

"Just made it," Nick said as the man fell back into one of the seats.

The man turned to look at him, his hand moving to the black briefcase. "What?" he asked with a look of **suspicion**[1] in his eyes.

"The train. You **only just**[2] made it."

The man's expression softened, and he smiled. "Yeah, only just."

Then the conductor blew his whistle, and the train began to move, its slow rhythm gently encouraging Nick towards sleep.

As his eyes began to shut, he suddenly realised that he had seen the man at the next table somewhere before. Was he a writer? A musician? Nick was not sure.

But anyway, did it really matter? Because in less than two hours the man would be dead.

"Ladies and gentlemen..." The polite French accent of the attendant woke Nick from a light sleep.

At first he thought that they had already reached Paris, but then he noticed the nervous expressions on the faces of the other passengers.

"Why have we stopped?" asked the young man with the newspaper.

"It's nothing to worry about, I assure you. We have a small technical problem, and we have had to stop the train for just a few minutes."

"What kind of problem?" asked the American, a tall man with a bald head and pink cheeks.

1 **suspicion** - *Misstrauen*
2 **only just** - *gerade noch*

"A minor problem with the electronics. Everything will be resolved in a moment."

"And where exactly are we? Under the bloody channel. Great place to break down," said the younger man again.

"Don't, James," said his wife.

"Sir, we have not broken down. The engine is fine; we just need to make a small repair," the attendant looked around at the nervous faces. "However, despite the fact that it is only a minor problem, we may lose the electricity in the carriages for a few minutes."

"Jesus Christ!" said the American. "You mean we're going to have to sit here in the dark?"

"For the briefest of moments, yes, but then the emergency lights will activate. And I can assure you it will take no more than a few minutes for the repairs to be completed."

There were no more questions, and the attendant took the opportunity to quickly retreat.

Leaning back in his seat Nick heard the man with the black briefcase at the next table swear. "Just when I thought I was out of the bloody country!"

"I'm sure it won't take long," said Nick.

"Yeah, well I know what will help with the wait," the man replied. Then, quickly turning the **dials**[1] on the lock of his briefcase, he opened it and removed a small silver **hip flask**[2]. "Best whisky money can buy," he grinned, and then he opened the flask and drank deeply. "Want some?"

Nick smiled. "I'm okay, thanks."

The man shook his head. "It won't kill you."

Then the lights flickered, and Nick looked around the carriage at the nervous faces.

"I think everything's okay," James said.

And that was when the darkness descended upon them.

1 **dial** - *Ziffer*
2 **hip flask** - *Flachmann*

Yes, the darkness was cold, consuming and complete, but the silence was not.

In fact, as Nick listened, he was sure that he could hear someone moving.

Someone **creeping**[1] along the carriage.

Someone breathing not far from him.

He turned his head to the left. Was that the shape of someone standing in the aisle by his table?

Someone waiting, watching?

Or was it just the dread of the tunnel, and the darkness playing tricks on his mind?

"Hello?" he asked. "Is someone there?"

And that was when the scream filled the silence.

It was a horrible sound: long, loud and barely human.

Panicked voices exploded from every part of the carriage, and Nick desperately pushed himself back against the window. "Lights!" he shouted. "Someone use a light. A phone, a torch, anything!"

"I've got my phone!" he heard James reply.

"Quickly!" Nick said, listening to the hurried movements in the darkness, sure that someone was moving towards him, trying to silence him.

But then the emergency lights activated, and the scene was **drenched**[2] in their strange glow.

Nick looked around.

There was no one in the aisle.

There was no one moving towards him.

"Who was that? Who screamed?" the American asked. "What the hell happened?"

Nick stood up. "I don't know. I think..." he began to say. But then he saw the body.

1 **to creep** - *kriechen*
2 **drenched** - *durchtränkt*

The eyes were open in a horrible expression of shock. Other than this, though, the man in the white shirt looked perfectly normal.

Apart from the small black knife **protruding**[1] from his chest.

"Jesus Christ!" said the American. Then his wife looked too, and another scream filled the carriage.

Nick watched as one by one the different passengers saw the body. The young couple were silent but horrified, both of them moving from their seats to stand in the aisle. The elderly lady looked at the knife then fell back into her seat, the Americans moving to help her as she **fainted**[2]. Behind him the two men in dark suits were talking, their expressions hard to read, and at the far end of the carriage the French woman was standing, her eyes moving across the faces of the other men and women.

"We've got to get out of here, Sian!" James said to the young woman, pulling her to the end of the carriage and hitting the button for the electric doors at the end of the aisle to open. "It's not working!" he shouted, hitting the button again.

"What do you mean?" asked the American.

"I mean it won't open! What else can that mean?"

"This one isn't working either," said the French lady from the other end of the carriage.

"What's... what's happening?" asked the elderly woman as her eyes flickered open.

"It's okay," Cherie, the American's wife, said, moving to her and holding her hand. "There's been... an accident."

"Accident?" said her husband. "The man's got a knife in his chest! Someone's murdered him!"

The words cut through the panic, and for a moment there was silence.

"Murdered?" repeated the elderly lady, but then her eyes rolled back into her head as she fainted again.

1 **to protrude from sth.** – *aus etw. hervorragen*
2 **to faint** – *ohnmächtig werden*

"Larry! Don't say that!" Cherie shouted at her husband.

"But he's right," said the French woman. "And there's something else which you should **consider**[1]."

Nick looked at her. "I know."

"What?" asked James. "What do you know?"

"Think about it. The lights went out because they cut the electricity to do the repairs."

"So?"

"So that's why the doors won't open either. They cut the power, the lights went out, the doors locked... and this man was murdered. Which means," continued the French woman, "that the murderer is still in this carriage." She looked around at the other passengers, watching their faces. "The murderer is one of you."

For a moment no one replied as each person searched the faces of the others.

"What the hell do you mean 'one of you'?" Larry shouted. "You're in here too! It could be you!"

The French woman shrugged. "Yes, but I know that it wasn't me."

"Look, we have to be calm about this," Nick said. "It won't be long until the electricity is turned on again. We just need to wait."

The French woman nodded. "I agree."

"Be calm? Wait?" asked James. "You just told us that someone in here is a murderer. Are we supposed to just wait until they kill someone else?"

Nick shook his head. "I don't think that's going to happen."

"Why not?" asked the French woman, taking a cigarette from her pocket and lighting it.

"Er, I don't think you can smoke in here," said Cherie.

"And I don't think you can kill people either, but look" she said and nodded at the body.

1 **to consider sth.** - *etw. in Betracht ziehen*

Behind him Nick could hear the two men in suits quietly talking, and he saw Larry look at them suspiciously. “What the hell are those two **jabbering**[1] about?”

The two men stopped talking, and one of them turned to Larry. “Excuse me?”

“Oh, so you do speak English. Maybe you could speak a bit more of it.”

The man's expression turned cold. “I speak English, but my colleague does not. And tell me, why should I speak English? Why don't you try speaking my language?”

Larry wiped the sweat from his head and sat down.

“You said you didn't think anyone else would be killed,” asked the French woman. “Why?”

Nick shook his head. “I don't know. There was something about this guy. When he got onto the train, I remember thinking that he looked nervous.”

“What?” asked James. “Like he knew someone wanted to kill him?”

“Maybe not kill him, but something.” Nick looked at the dead man's face again, and that feeling that he recognised him returned. “Does anyone know this man?”

Larry shrugged. “You were the one talking to him.”

“No, I mean, his face. Is it familiar?”

Everyone turned to look at the body, but one by one they turned their eyes from him.

“Wait!” Sian said, standing up and staring. “I do! I recognise him. He was in James' newspaper!”

James moved back to their table and picked up the forgotten paper. “Jesus, you're right. He's here on the second bloody page.

“Who is he?”

1 **to jabber** – *quasseln*

"It says he's some ex-butler for some upper-class family. Jesus, yeah, it says this family is basically an extended part of the royal family. Some of the richest people in the country."

"Why ex-butler?" asked the French woman, **extinguishing**[1] her cigarette beneath her shoe.

"It says the family suspected him of stealing but could never prove it."

"So what does all this mean?" Larry asked. "It doesn't explain who killed him."

James shook his head. "It might, actually. The article says this guy **claimed**[2] to have some photos of the eldest son of the family. Apparently these pictures show him doing some pretty awful things, and they could ruin the family's reputation forever."

Nick looked at the dead man, and then let his eyes move to the black briefcase.

"The pictures must be in the case. If we can see them, maybe we will know who killed him," and he looked around at the others. "Does anyone disagree?"

There was a feeling of tension in the carriage again now, but no one spoke. He turned to the two men in dark suits and waited until the interpreter nodded his head in consent.

"I suppose waiting would have been boring," the French woman said. She moved down the aisle towards them. Larry and Cherie got up from their seats and stepped closer too.

"Who'll open it?" asked Sian.

Nick shrugged. "I'll do it, if I can get this lock open."

"Try this," James said, passing him a small **penknife**[3] that was attached to his keys.

Nick looked around once more, sure that whoever wanted the pictures to remain secret would say something.

1 **to extinguish sth.** - *etw. löschen, etw. ausmachen*
2 **to claim sth.** - *etw. behaupten*
3 **penknife** - *Taschenmesser*

Then, turning the case towards him he slid the small **blunt**[1] knife between the first lock and twisted it, the metal breaking easily.

"You know," said James. "Whatever is in there could make us rich."

Nick shook his head. "I just want to know who killed him."

He put the knife under the second lock and was about to turn when suddenly the emergency lights flickered.

"Jesus, if they turn off too..." James began.

Then the darkness swallowed them once more.

The first scream he heard was Sian's. Nick was sure of that, but he did not know if it was the loss of the lights or something much worse. The second scream, however, came from Larry.

And it was a scream of pain.

All around him voices filled the darkness with fear and panic; then something hard hit him around the head, and he fell back, dizzy and confused.

"The briefcase," a voice shouted. "Get the briefcase!"

Nick felt hands push him away, but he was angry now, the anger suffocating the fear. He swung his right arm, but there was nothing there. He swung the left, and his fist smashed against skin and bone.

"Bastard!" a voice shouted in the darkness.

"Lights! James, get the lights!"

For a moment there was nothing, but then bright white lights appeared from James' phone and then from Sian's and the interpreter's.

The scene was chaotic.

James had been pushed to the floor, and there was blood on his head where it had struck a table. Larry was lying on two seats and groaning, another small knife pushed into his shoulder.

1 **blunt** – *stumpf*

And in front of Nick, his nose pouring with blood, was the train attendant.

"You?" Nick shouted. "Why?"

The attendant shook his head. "She paid me! She said all I had to do was cut the lights and make it seem like the doors were locked. She said no one would know. That no one would suspect her, and she would escape and never tell anyone I helped. I needed the money you see."

"She?" Nick spun round, his eyes scanning the carriage.

Both sets of doors were now open.

And the French woman was gone.

"James, keep him here." Nick ran along the aisle and through the carriage doors. He then stopped and stared out of the open **exterior door**[1].

It was dark out there, the only **illumination**[2] provided by dim grey lights, and he had no idea if the French woman was waiting for him with another knife.

For a brief moment he hesitated. Then he jumped out of the door into the tunnel, turned to his left and ran into the darkness.

"Where are you going?" he heard the French woman say from behind him.

He turned to her slowly, raising his own hands and expecting to see a weapon in hers.

"Ha!" she laughed. "You thought it was me? How **gullible**[3] you are. I felt her push past me. I didn't know who it was until I caught her out here. I suppose my face probably looked as shocked as yours."

Nick lowered his hands and shook his head. "I don't believe it. Why?"

1. **exterior door** - *Außentür*
2. **illumination** - *Beleuchtung*
3. **gullible** - *naiv*

The elderly woman was silent for a moment, her arms held firmly behind her back by the French woman. Her lace hat was gone, and her thin dark hair was a mess. By her feet was another knife which Nick guessed the French woman had taken from her.

When she spoke, her voice was cold and bitter. "Why? You ask me that?" she **shrieked**[1], her tone hinting at some type of mania. "That man deserved to die. He was a thief and a liar. More than that, though, he betrayed one of the oldest and noblest families in the country. I would do it again in an instant."

"Who are you?" asked Nick. "You can't be part of the family or he would have recognised you."

The woman shook her head, her old eyes half-**crazed**[2]. "Oh, but I am part of the family. One of the most important parts. I looked after the boy like a mother. I protected him from **scum**[3] like that dead man all his young life. And yes, they took my job from me when they said I was too old, but that doesn't mean I just **give in**[4]. It doesn't mean I just stop loving him. I had enough money saved up to pay that idiot attendant to stop the train. I would have paid every penny I had. Because I knew the family would thank me. I knew my little lord would thank me. Because I could kill that thief and go to prison, and the family could keep its reputation."

Nick shook his head again.

"Englishman, it's not hard to see, is it?" the French woman said with a raised eyebrow. "Our sweet little old lady is our rich lord's nanny."

1 **to shriek** - *kreischen*
2 **crazed** - *wirr*
3 **scum** - *Abschaum*
4 **to give in** - *aufgeben*

Für den Channel Tunnel (Deutsch: Eurotunnel) gab es bereits im 18. Jahrhundert erste Ideen, wobei diese damals noch die Fortbewegung mittels Pferdekutschen vorsahen mit einer Insel in der Mitte des durch Öllampen erleuchteten Tunnels, die dem Tausch der Pferde dienen sollte.

1987 begannen die Arbeiten am Tunnel, an denen insgesamt 13.000 Arbeiter, Techniker und Ingenieure beteiligt waren. Nach der Fertigstellung 1994 war es zum ersten Mal seit dem Ende der letzten Eiszeit vor über 13.000 Jahren möglich, trockenen Fußes vom europäischen Festland nach Großbritannien zu gelangen.

Der Eurotunnel ist im Laufe der Jahre immer wieder Ausgangspunkt für zahlreiche Flüchtlinge, die durch den Tunnel ins Vereinigte Königreich gelangen wollen, indem sie versuchen, auf LKWs und Güterzüge zu klettern. Dabei kommt es immer wieder zu Todesfällen.

WORTLISTE

Verwendete Abkürzungen

AE = amerikanisches Englisch
AUS = australisches Englisch
BE = britisches Englisch
etw. = etwas
jd. = jemand
jdm. = jemandem
jdn.= jemanden
jds.= jemandes
pl. = Plural
sb. = somebody
sth. = something
ugs. = umgangssprachlich

	abandoned	*verlassen*
to	**abuse sb.**	*jdn. misshandeln*
	accelerator	*Gaspedal*
	access point	*Zugangspunkt*
	acquaintance	*Bekanntschaft*
	ad	*Anzeige*
to	**add**	*hinzufügen*
to	**adjust**	*zurechtrücken*
to	**adjust to sth.**	*sich an etw. gewöhnen*
to	**affect**	*beeinflussen*
	agreement	*Vereinbarung*
	aisle	*Gang*
	All I need to do is shout.	*Ich brauche nur zu schreien.*
	All rise!	*Bitte erheben Sie sich!*
	although	*obgleich*
	amazement	*Erstaunen*
	ambassador	*Botschafter*
	amount	*Summe*
	amusing	*amüsierend*
	ancestor	*Vorfahr*
	... and that's final.	*... und dabei bleibt es.*
	annoyance	*Ärger, Verärgerung*
	annoyed	*verärgert*
	antidote	*Gegengift*
	anxiety	*Unbehagen*
	anything but	*nichts anderes als*
	apologetic	*entschuldigend*
to	**apologise**	*um Entschuldigung bitten*
	apology	*Entschuldigung*
	argument	*Streit*
	arson	*Brandstiftung*
	As soon as that command is given...	*Sobald dieser Befehl erteilt wird...*
	as though	*als ob*
	assassination	*Ermordung*
to	**assess sb.**	*jdn. mustern*
	at first	*zuerst*
	ATM (Automated Teller Machine) *(AE)*	*Geldautomat*
	atmospheric	*stimmungsvoll*
to	**atone for sth.**	*für etw. büßen*
	attempted murder	*versuchter Mord*
	attendant	*Zugbegleiter; Wärter*
	auburn	*rostrot*
	authority	*Behörde*
	available	*verfügbar*
	awake	*munter*
to	**awake**	*aufwachen*
	awesome *(AE)*	*super*
	awkward silence	*betretenes Schweigen*
	aye *(Schottisch)*	*ja*
	badge with her name	*Namensschild*
to	**bang against sth.**	*gegen etw. stoßen*
	baseball bat	*Baseballschläger*
to	**be about to do sth.**	*im Begriff sein, etw. zu tun*

to	**be asleep**	*schlafen*
to	**be aware**	*merken*
to	**be convicted of a crime**	*eines Verbrechens überführt werden*
to	**be devoid of sth.**	*an etw. mangeln*
to	**be in no rush**	*es nicht eilig haben*
to	**be in one's prime**	*im besten Alter sein*
to	**be mistaken**	*sich irren*
to	**be sore**	*weh tun*
to	**be terrified**	*schreckliche Angst vor etw. haben*
to	**be the one**	*der/die Richtige sein*
	bead of sweat	*Schweißperle*
to	**beat**	*schlagen*
	bedside table	*Nachttisch*
to	**bet**	*wetten*
to	**betray sb.**	*jdn. verraten*
	bill *(AE)*	*Geldschein*
	billboard	*Reklametafel*
	binoculars (pl.)	*Fernglas*
to	**blackmail sb.**	*jdn. erpressen*
to	**blame sb. for sth.**	*jdm. etw. verübeln*
	blank	*ausdruckslos*
to	**blaze**	*funkeln*
	blind drunk	*stockbetrunken*
	blistering	*glühend*
	bloke	*Typ*
	bloody *(AUS, BE)*	*verdammt*
	blunt	*stumpf*
to	**blush**	*erröten*
	body	*Leiche*
	body bag	*Leichensack*
	boot	*Stiefel*
to	**bother**	*stören*
to	**bow**	*sich verbeugen*
	box	*Loge*
	brave	*mutig*
to	**bray**	*wiehern; kreischen*
	breath	*Atem*
	breeze	*Brise*
to	**brew**	*brauen*
	brick	*Baustein*
	brief	*kurz*
to	**bring sb. to justice**	*jdn. vor Gericht bringen*

	broad	*breit gebaut*
	bruise	*Bluterguss*
	buck *(AE)*	*Dollar*
	building work	*Bauarbeiten*
	bullet-proof vest	*schusssichere Weste*
to	**bump into sb.**	*mit jdm. zusammenstoßen*
	burglar	*Einbrecher(in)*
	burial stone	*Grabstein*
	burn	*Brandwunde*
	cabin	*Hütte*
to	**call for sb. to do sth.**	*jdn. auffordern, etw. zu tun*
	canteen	*Mensa*
	capable	*tüchtig*
	capacity	*Potential*
	carriage	*Wagen*
to	**cause sth.**	*etw. verursachen*
	cellmate	*Zellengenosse*
	CEO (Chief Executive Officer)	*Geschäftsführer(in)*
	chained	*angekettet*
	chamber	*Amtskammer*
	change	*Kleingeld*
to	**chase**	*verfolgen*
to	**cheat**	*schummeln*
to	**cheat on sb.**	*jdn. betrügen*
	chess board	*Schachbrett*
	chest	*Brust*
	chief inspector	*Hauptkommissar*
	chipped and bitten	*eingerissen und abgekaut*
	Christ! *(ugs.)*	*Um Gottes willen!*
to	**claim a life insurance**	*Anprüche aus einer Lebensversicherung geltend machen*
to	**claim sth.**	*etw. behaupten*
	class	*Unterricht*
to	**climb**	*klettern*
	closet *(AE)*	*Kleiderschrank*
	club	*Knüppel*
	cockroach	*Kakerlake*
	coffin	*Sarg*
	coil of rope	*Seilrolle*
to	**collapse**	*einstürzen*

to	**come to do sth.**	*dazu kommen, etw. zu tun*
	comforting	*beruhigend*
	commuter	*Pendler(in)*
	companion	*Begleiter(in)*
	comparison	*Vergleich*
	competitor	*Konkurrent(in)*
to	**compose oneself**	*sich zusammennehmen*
	comprehensive school	*Gesamtschule*
to	**con sb.** *(ugs.)*	*jdn. betrügen*
	concerned	*besorgt*
	condo(minium) *(AE)*	*Eigentumswohnung*
	conductor	*Schaffner(in)*
to	**confess**	*ein Geständnis ablegen*
	confession	*Geständnis*
	confused	*irritiert*
	confusion	*Verwirrung*
	conservatory	*Wintergarten*
to	**consider sth.**	*etw. in Betracht ziehen*
	constable	*Polizist*
to	**contemplate**	*erwägen*
	content	*zufrieden*
	Conus geographus	*Landkartenkegel*
	convict	*Sträfling; Strafgefangene(r)*
	cop *(AE, ugs.)*	*Bulle*
	cop shop *(AUS, ugs.)*	*Polizeiwache*
	copycat killer	*Nachahmungstäter*
	corner shop	*Tante-Emma-Laden*
	coroner	*Gerichtsmediziner*
	corridor	*Flur*
	cosy	*gemütlich*
	cotton mill	*Baumwollspinnerei*
	couple	*Paar*
	court clerk	*Gerichtsdiener*
	courtroom	*Gerichtssaal*
	courtyard	*Innenhof*
	coz *(ugs.)*	*weil*
	crack	*Spalt*
to	**crack a case**	*einen Fall lösen*
	crackle	*Knistern*
	crazed	*wirr*
	crazy	*verrückt*
to	**creak**	*knarren*
to	**creep**	*kriechen*
	cricket	*Grille*
	crime novel	*Kriminalroman*
	crowded	*voller Menschen*
	crown court	*Strafgerichtshof*
	cruel	*grausam*
	cruise	*Kreuzfahrt*
to	**crush**	*mahlen, zerkleinern*
to	**cry out**	*aufschreien*
to	**cuff sb. to sth.**	*jdn. mit Handschellen an etw. fesseln*
to	**cycle**	*Rad fahren*
	dagger	*Dolch*
	damp	*feucht*
to	**dare**	*wagen*
	darkness	*Dunkelheit*
	deafening	*ohrenbetäubend*
	dear	*Schatz (auch unter Fremden)*
	death anniversary	*Todestag*
	deceased	*verstorben; Verstorbene(r)*
	deed	*Tat*
	defeated	*besiegt*
	defence	*Verteidigung*
to	**defend oneself**	*sich verteidigen*
	defendant	*Angeklagte(r)*
	defensively	*verteidigend*
	defiant	*unnachgiebig*
	demeanour	*Auftreten*
	derelict	*verlassen*
	deserted	*verlassen*
	desperately	*verzweifelt*
	despite	*trotz*
to	**destroy**	*vernichten*
to	**detect**	*entdecken*
	deterrent	*Abschreckung*
	devotion	*Ergebenheit*
	dial	*Ziffer*
	Did he hell! *(ugs.)*	*Nie im Leben!*
to	**disappear into thin air**	*sich in Luft auflösen*
	disgraced	*blamiert*
	disguise	*Tarnung*

	disgust	*Ekel*
to	**dismiss sth./sb. from one's thoughts**	*etw./jdn. ausblenden*
	disquieting	*beunruhigend*
	distaste	*Abneigung*
	distorted	*verzerrt*
	distraction	*Ablenkung*
	dizzy	*schwindlig*
	domed	*gewölbt*
	domestic abuse	*häusliche Gewalt*
	donkey	*Esel*
	Don't you dare!	*Wage es nicht!*
	doorbell	*Türklingel*
	doubtless	*sicherlich*
to	**down a drink**	*ein Getränk austrinken*
to	**downsize**	*schrumpfen*
	Do you mind?	*Stört es Sie?*
to	**drag**	*schleifen*
	dread	*Grauen, Furcht*
	drenched	*durchtränkt*
	dressing gown	*Bademantel*
to	**drip**	*tropfen*
	driveway	*Auffahrt; Einfahrt*
to	**drop (off) sth.**	*abliefern*
	drug	*Medikament*
	due to	*infolge*
	dull	*stumpf*
	dust	*Staub*
to	**echo**	*widerhallen*
	edge	*Rand*
to	**edge forward**	*sich langsam vorwärtsbewegen*
	editor	*Herausgeber(in); Redakteur(in)*
	effort	*Bemühung*
	either… or	*entweder… oder*
	elaborate	*kunstvoll*
	elderly	*älter*
	elevator *(AE)*	*Aufzug*
	embassy	*Botschaft*
	encounter	*Begegnung*
	enemy	*Feind*
	enough	*genug*
to	**enter a property by force**	*einbrechen*
	entire	*ganz, gesamt*
to	**escape**	*fliehen*
	evidence	*Beweis*
	excavation	*Ausgrabung*
	except for	*bis auf*
	exhausted	*erschöpft*
	expat	*im Ausland lebender Mensch*
to	**expect**	*erwarten*
	expression	*Gesichtsausdruck*
	exterior door	*Außentür*
to	**extinguish sth.**	*etw. (aus)löschen; etw. ausmachen*
	extremely	*äußerst*
to	**fade**	*schwinden*
to	**fail to do sth.**	*etw. nicht machen können*
to	**faint**	*ohnmächtig werden*
	fake	*falsch*
to	**fall asleep**	*einschlafen*
to	**fall for sb.**	*jdm. verfallen*
	familiar	*vertraut*
to	**familiarise oneself with sth.**	*sich mit etw. vertraut machen*
the	**family**	*die „Familie": amerikanisch-italienische Mafia*
	fault	*Schuld*
	fault in the system	*Systemfehler*
	fear	*Angst*
to	**feel a stab of jealousy**	*einen Anflug von Eifersucht verspüren*
to	**feel ill**	*sich krank fühlen*
to	**feel like doing sth.**	*Lust haben, etw. zu tun*
to	**feel one's legs go weak**	*weiche Knie bekommen*
to	**feel sympathy for sb.**	*mit jdm. Mitleid haben*
	female lead	*weibliche Hauptrolle*
	fence	*Zaun*
to	**fight**	*kämpfen*
	figure	*Gestalt*

	filing cabinet	*Aktenschrank*
	filthy	*dreckig*
	fire engine	*Feuerwehrauto*
	flaky	*bröckelig*
	flammable	*leichtentzündlich*
	flare	*Leuchtfackel*
to	**flash sth.**	*etw. aufblitzen lassen*
	flask	*Flachmann*
to	**flee**	*flüchten*
to	**flick through sth.**	*etw. durchblättern*
to	**flicker**	*flimmern*
	foot	*Fuß (0,3048 Meter)*
	footstep	*Schritt*
	for	*denn*
	for his amusement	*zu seinem Vergnügen*
	fortified wine	*Dessertwein*
	fortune	*Vermögen*
	foster family	*Pflegefamilie*
	foul	*grauenhaft*
to	**frame sb. for sth.**	*jdm. etw. anhängen*
to	**freeze**	*erstarren*
	freezer	*Gefriertruhe*
	fright	*Erschrecken*
	front desk	*Empfang*
to	**frown**	*die Stirn runzeln*
	funeral	*Beerdigung*
	furious	*zornig*
	G'day! *(AUS)*	*Guten Tag!*
	gag	*Knebel*
to	**gag**	*knebeln*
	gambling addiction	*Spielsucht*
	gasp	*Keuchen*
to	**get** *(BE, ugs.)*	*verstehen*
to	**get hurt**	*verletzt werden*
to	**get involved in sth.**	*in etw. verwickelt werden*
to	**get life**	*lebenslänglich bekommen*
to	**get revenge**	*sich rächen*
to	**get sth. wrapped up**	*etw. eingetütet bekommen (zum Abschluss bringen)*
to	**get the hell out of this city**	*aus dieser Stadt abhauen*
	ghastliness	*Grässlichkeit*
	giant	*Riese*
to	**give in**	*aufgeben*
to	**give sb. a slap**	*jdm. eine Ohrfeige geben*
	glow	*Glühen*
to	**go**	*hier: sterben*
to	**go wrong**	*schiefgehen*
	goddamn	*verdammt*
	Good job I've quit.	*Zum Glück habe ich aufgehört.*
	gorgeous	*umwerfend*
	gossip	*Tratsch*
	gown	*Talar*
to	**grab sth.**	*sich etw. schnappen*
	grammar school	*Gymnasium*
	grand (pl.) *(ugs.)*	*(Geldscheine) Riesen, Tausender*
	grim	*düster*
	grin	*Grinsen*
to	**grin**	*grinsen*
to	**groan**	*stöhnen*
	groin	*Leiste*
	grounds (pl.)	*Anlagen*
to	**grow sth.**	*etw. anbauen*
	growl	*Knurren*
to	**growl**	*anknurren*
	guilt	*Schuldgefühl*
	guilty	*schuldig*
	gullible	*naiv*
	gurney *(AE)*	*Rollbahre*
	hammer of the pistol	*Hahn der Pistole*
to	**handcuff sb. to sth.**	*jdn. mit Handschellen an etw. fesseln*
	handset	*Hörer*
to	**hate**	*hassen*
to	**head towards sth.**	*sich auf etw. zubewegen*
	headmaster	*Schulleiter*
	heaps of sth. *(ugs.)*	*ein ganzer Haufen einer Sache, sehr viele*
	hearing	*Hörvermögen*
	heartbroken	*untröstlich*
to	**heave**	*würgen*
	Here's to you.	*Auf dein Wohl.*

to	**hesitate**	*zögern*
	He would find...	*Er würde finden...*
	hidden	*versteckt*
to	**hide**	*verbergen*
	highway	*Schnellstraße*
to	**hike**	*wandern*
	hillside	*Berghang*
	hip flask	*Flachmann*
to	**hiss**	*zischen*
to	**hit**	*schlagen*
	hit-and-run accident	*Unfall mit Fahrerflucht*
to	**hit the bar** *(ugs.)*	*zur Bar gehen*
	homicide	*Tötung*
	hood	*Kapuze*
	horrendous	*entsetzlich*
	horrible	*schrecklich*
	horror	*Entsetzen*
	housemate	*Mitbewohner(in)*
to	**hover**	*schweben*
	How dare you?	*Wie können Sie es wagen?*
	How the hell would I know? *(ugs.)*	*Woher zum Teufel soll ich das wissen?*
	humid	*schwül*
	hunting lodge	*Jagdhütte*
to	**hurt sb.**	*jdm. wehtun*
	hushed	*gedämpft*
	icicle	*Eiszapfen*
	I could have killed you then.	*Ich hätte dich dann umbringen können.*
	I dinna ken aboot that. Better the morra. *(Schottisch)*	*Ich weiß nicht. Lieber morgen.*
	idly	*träge*
	I don't suppose you can change a twenty?	*Könnten Sie einen Zwanziger wechseln?*
	I don't think so.	*Ich glaube nicht.*
	If you have to.	*Wenn du musst.*
to	**ignite**	*anzünden*
to	**illuminate**	*beleuchten*
	illuminated	*erhellt*
	illumination	*Beleuchtung*
	immaculately	*makellos*
	impatience	*Ungeduld*
	impenetrable	*undurchdringlich*
	impressive	*imposant*
	inability	*Unfähigkeit*
	in a sane state of mind	*zurechnungsfähig*
	incendiary	*Brandmittel*
	indeed	*durchaus*
	in disbelief	*ungläubig*
	in distress	*in der Not*
	in fact	*eigentlich*
	influence	*Einfluss, Beziehungen*
to	**inherit sth.**	*etw. erben*
	injury	*Verletzung*
	ink	*Tinte*
	ink cartridge	*Tintenpatrone*
	in mysterious circumstances	*unter mysteriösen Umständen*
	innocent	*unschuldig*
	inquest	*Untersuchungsausschuss*
	in regards to	*bezüglich*
	insane	*verrückt*
	insistent	*hartnäckig; beharrlich*
	in spite of the fact	*trotz der Tatsache*
	instantly	*augenblicklich*
	instead	*stattdessen*
	insulted	*beleidigt*
to	**intend to**	*beabsichtigen*
	in this very house	*in ebendiesem Haus*
	intruder	*Einbrecher(in)*
	I see.	*Ich verstehe.*
	I suppose we can...	*Wir können wohl...*
	It feels like...	*Es fühlt sich an wie...*
	its very absence	*eben ihre/seine Abwesenheit*
	I would hear...	*Ich hörte immer ...*
	I would rather...	*Ich würde lieber...*
to	**jabber**	*quasseln*
	jet-black	*samtschwarz*
	jetty	*Pier*
	journey	*Fahrt*
	jug	*Krug*

	kernel	*Kern*
to	**kneel down**	*sich hinknien*
	knitting needle	*Stricknadel*
	knitting things	*Strickzeug*
	lace hat	*Hut aus Spitze*
	ladies	*Damentoilette*
to	**lament over sth.**	*über etw. klagen*
	landing	*Treppenabsatz*
	larder	*Speisekammer*
	late	*hier: verstorben*
to	**laugh at sb.**	*jdn. auslachen*
	laughter	*Gelächter*
	lazy	*faul*
	lead	*Hinweis*
to	**lean down**	*sich beugen*
to	**leave**	*verlassen*
to	**leave sb. alone**	*jdn. in Ruhe lassen*
to	**leave sth. to sb.**	*jdm. etw. hinterlassen*
	length	*Länge*
	lenient	*nachsichtig*
	letter opener	*Brieföffner*
	licence	*Führerschein*
	lid	*Deckel*
to	**lie**	*liegen*
	Like father like son.	*Wie der Vater, so der Sohn.*
to	**line**	*säumen*
	loan request	*Darlehensantrag*
	lobby	*Eingangshalle*
	location	*Stelle*
	loch *(Schottisch)*	*See*
	lodge	*Hütte*
to	**look forward to sth.**	*sich auf etw. freuen*
to	**lose one's mind**	*den Verstand verlieren*
	lounge	*Salon*
	lovely	*entzückend*
	lumber yard	*Holzlager*
	lumberjack shirt	*Holzfällerhemd*
	luminous hands	*Leuchtzeiger*
	lump	*Beule*
	luv	*Schatz (Kosename verwendet in Yorskshire auch unter fremden Leuten)*
	madman	*Verrückter*
	magnifying glass	*Lupe*
	maid	*Dienstmädchen*
to	**make a fist**	*eine Faust machen*
to	**make notes**	*Notizen machen*
to	**make sb.'s hair stand up**	*jdm. die Haare zu Berge stehen lassen*
to	**make sb.'s life hell**	*jdm. das Leben zur Hölle machen*
to	**manage to do sth.**	*es schaffen, etw. zu tun*
	manor (house)	*Herrenhaus*
	manslaughter	*Totschlag*
	many a tale	*manch eine Geschichte*
to	**match**	*übereinstimmen, passen*
	mate	*Kumpel*
	menacing	*bedrohlich*
	mental *(ugs.)*	*übergeschnappt*
	mercy	*Gnade*
	mess	*Durcheinander*
	messy	*unordentlich*
	metal spring	*Metallfeder*
	middle-aged	*mittleren Alters*
	miraculously	*wie durch ein Wunder*
	misery	*Elend*
	missing person	*vermisste Person*
	mistake	*Fehler*
	mistrust	*Misstrauen*
	moan	*Stöhnen*
	mobile (phone)	*Handy*
to	**mock sth.**	*etw. verspotten*
	mocking	*spöttisch*
	moor	*Heideland*
	mop handle	*Wischmophalter*
	most of	*die meisten*
	motionless	*regungslos*
	muddy stain	*Schlammfleck*
	muffled	*gedämpft*
	multitude	*Vielzahl*
	murder scene	*Tatort*
	Murder will out.	*Der Täter wird erwischt. / Die Wahrheit wird herauskommen.*

to	mute	*dämpfen*
	muted	*gedämpft*
to	narrow	*sich verengen*
	nearby	*in der Nähe*
	neat	*ordentlich*
	Neither.	*Weder noch.*
	neither... nor	*weder... noch*
	next of kin	*nächster Angehöriger*
	nobody but	*niemand außer*
	Nobody seemed to notice that...	*Niemand schien zu bemerken, dass...*
to	nod	*mit dem Kopf nicken*
	noise	*Geräusch*
	none	*keine*
	nope *(ugs.)*	*nö*
	notepad	*Notizblock*
	not to have a clue	*keine Ahnung haben*
	not to leave a spot	*sich nicht vom Fleck rühren*
	novel	*Roman*
	novelist	*Schriftsteller(in)*
	nowhere near closed	*längst nicht abgeschlossen*
	number plate	*Nummernschild*
	oak	*Eiche*
	oar	*Ruder*
to	observe	*beobachten*
	occasionally	*gelegentlich*
	ocean liner	*Ozeandampfer*
	odd	*seltsam*
	Oh my!	*Meine Güte!*
	Oh my gosh!	*Oh mein Gott!*
	one's true self	*jds. wahres Ich*
	only just	*gerade noch*
	opportunity	*Gelegenheit*
	opposite	*gegenüber*
	ordinary	*herkömmlich, gewöhnlich*
	outskirts *(pl.)*	*Stadtrand*
	paint	*Lack*
	pair of scissors	*Schere*
	pal	*Kumpel*
	pale	*hell*
	pants *(AE, pl.)*	*Hose*
	paramedic	*Sanitäter(in)*
	passage	*Gang*
	peat bog	*Torfmoor*
	penknife	*Taschenmesser*

	perimeter	*Stadtrand*
	perpetrator	*Täter(in)*
	petty criminal	*Kleinkriminelle(r)*
	picture	*Foto*
	piece of cloth	*Stoffstück*
	PIN	*Geheimzahl*
	plain	*unscheinbar*
	plate	*Nummernschild*
	pleasant	*angenehm*
	plot	*Handlung*
to	plunge sth. into sth.	*etw. in etw. hineinstecken*
	poison	*Gift*
to	poison	*vergiften*
	polish	*Politur*
	politely	*höflich*
	poor thing	*armes Ding*
	porch *(AE)*	*Veranda*
	power cut	*Stromausfall*
	premeditated murder	*vorsätzlicher Mord*
	premises *(pl.)*	*Grundstück*
to	prescribe	*verschreiben*
	private man	*zurückhaltender Mann*
	procedure	*Standardprozedur*
	profit	*Gewinn*
	prosecution	*Staatsanwaltschaft*
to	protrude from sth.	*aus etw. hervorragen*
to	prove	*beweisen*
	puff	*Atemstoß*
to	pull an insurance job	*einen Versicherungsbetrug begehen*
to	pull oneself together	*sich zusammenreißen*
to	punish	*bestrafen*
	purse	*Geldbeutel*
	push	*Stoß, Schubs*
to	put a fire out	*ein Feuer löschen*
to	put the kettle on	*(Tee)wasser aufsetzen*
	quack *(AUS, ugs.)*	*Arzt*
	quaint	*urig*
	questioningly	*fragend*
to	race	*pochen*
to	raise	*heben*
	raw	*wund*
	razor wire	*Nato-Draht*

to	**reach sth. out to sb.**	*jdm. etw. hinstrecken*
to	**reach up to**	*bis… hinaufreichen*
	real	*echt*
	real player	*führende Figur*
to	**realise** *(BE)*, **realize**	*feststellen, merken; sich klar werden*
to	**recall sth.**	*sich an etw. erinnern*
to	**reckon** *(ugs.)*	*meinen, schätzen, glauben*
	recording device	*Aufnahmegerät*
	reed	*Schilf*
to	**refill sb.'s glass**	*jdm. nachschenken*
to	**refuse to**	*sich weigern*
	registration	*Kraftfahrzeugbrief*
	regret	*Reue*
	reinforced glass	*drahtverstärktes Glas*
	remain	*Rest*
	remote	*abgelegen*
	repellent	*widerwärtig*
to	**reply**	*antworten*
to	**rescue**	*retten*
to	**resist**	*Widerstand leisten*
to	**resist sb.'s charms**	*dem Charme von jdm. widerstehen*
	respiratory failure	*Atemversagen*
	respiratory system	*Atmungssystem*
to	**retch**	*würgen*
to	**retreat**	*sich zurückziehen*
	reverend	*Pastor*
to	**rewind**	*zurückspulen*
	ridiculous	*absurd*
	rim-to-river trek	*Wanderung vom Rand des Grand Canyons zum Colorado River*
to	**rip into sth.**	*etw. zerreißen*
	ripped	*zerrissen*
to	**rise**	*hinaufsteigen*
to	**rock**	*schaukeln*

to	**roll over**	*sich umdrehen*
	rope	*Seil*
to	**rot**	*verfaulen*
	routine check	*Routinekontrolle*
to	**row**	*rudern*
to	**rub**	*reiben*
	rubbish *(BE)*	*Müll*
	rubbish collector	*Müllabfuhr(wagen)*
	ruined flesh	*zerfetztes Fleisch*
	rules and regulations	*Regeln und Vorschriften*
	ruling	*Richterspruch, Gerichtsentscheid*
	safe	*ungefährlich; in Sicherheit*
	savage	*brutal*
	scaffolding	*Baugerüst*
	scar	*Narbe*
	scarecrow	*Vogelscheuche*
	scared	*verängstigt, ängstlich*
	school tie	*Krawatte der Schuluniform*
to	**scramble**	*hasten*
to	**scribble**	*kritzeln*
	scum	*Abschaum*
to	**search**	*durchsuchen*
	search party	*Suchtrupp*
	secure	*fest*
to	**seem**	*scheinen*
	sensation	*Gefühl*
	sense of impending doom	*Vernichtungsgefühl*
to	**sense sth.**	*etw. spüren*
to	**shake one's head**	*den Kopf schütteln*
	shame	*Schamgefühl*
	Shame.	*Wie schade.*
	shark	*Hai*
	sharp	*spitz*
	sharp pain	*stechender Schmerz*
	She is all that matters.	*Sie ist alles, worauf es mir ankommt.*
	She's only going to be one minute.	*Sie ist gleich da.*
	shift	*Schicht*

to	**shine the torch around**	*mit der Taschenlampe die Gegend ableuchten*
	shiver	*Schauder*
to	**shiver**	*erschaudern*
to	**shoot sb.**	*jdn. erschießen*
	shortly	*in Kürze*
	Shouldn't I...	*Sollte ich nicht...*
to	**shout**	*rufen*
to	**show sb. out**	*jdn. hinausbegleiten*
to	**show sb. to the door**	*jdn. zur Tür bringen*
to	**shriek**	*kreischen*
to	**shrug**	*mit den Achseln zucken*
	shyly	*schüchtern*
	sicko *(ugs.)*	*Geistesgestörte(r)*
	sigh	*Seufzen*
to	**sigh**	*seufzen*
to	**signal to sb.**	*jdm. ein Zeichen geben*
	silly	*albern*
to	**sink**	*versinken*
	Sir?	*Wie, bitte?*
to	**sit back**	*sich zurücklehnen*
to	**sit up**	*sich aufsetzen*
	skyscraper	*Wolkenkratzer*
to	**slap**	*klatschen*
	sleeping pill	*Schlaftablette*
	slight	*kaum vernehmbar*
to	**slow down**	*bremsen*
	smart	*schick*
	snail	*Schnecke*
	snap	*Schuss*
to	**snap**	*aufschnappen*
to	**snap at sb.**	*jdn. anfahren*
to	**soak**	*durchnässen*
	soaked	*pitschnass*
	soil	*Erde*
	solitary	*einsam*
	someone might come	*jd. könnte kommen*
	So what?	*Na und?*
	spare room	*Gästezimmer*
to	**speak up**	*lauter sprechen*
	Speaking of which...	*Da wir gerade davon reden, ...*

to	**speed**	*flitzen*
to	**split**	*aufteilen, spalten*
	spontaneous combustion	*spontane Verbrennung*
to	**spot sth. from a mile away**	*sofort erkennen*
to	**spread**	*sich ausbreiten*
to	**stab sb.**	*jdn. niederstechen*
	stack	*Stapel*
	stag	*Hirsch*
to	**stagger**	*schwanken*
	staircase	*Treppenhaus*
to	**stare at sth.**	*etw. anstarren*
to	**stay awake**	*munter bleiben*
to	**stay cool**	*ruhig bleiben*
	steering wheel	*Lenkrad*
	stew	*Eintopf*
	stock	*Aktie*
	stomach	*Bauch*
	strangely	*seltsam*
	strap	*Riemen*
	streak	*Strähne*
to	**stretch out**	*sich ausstrecken*
to	**strike sb./sth.**	*jdn./gegen etw. schlagen*
to	**stroll**	*schlendern*
	struggle	*Kampf*
	Struth! *(AUS, ugs.)*	*Mensch!*
	studiously	*sorgsam*
	study	*Arbeitszimmer*
	stunned	*verblüfft*
	subtle	*dezent*
	subway *(AE)*	*U-Bahn*
	suddenly	*plötzlich*
to	**suffer**	*leiden*
to	**suffocate**	*ersticken*
to	**suggest**	*vorschlagen*
to	**suit sb.**	*jdm. (gut) stehen (Kleidung)*
	sunrise	*Sonnenaufgang*
	support	*Stütze*
to	**suppose**	*vermuten*
to	**suppress the image**	*die Vorstellung unterdrücken*
	Sure! *(ugs.)*	*Klar!*
	surely	*bestimmt*
to	**surround**	*umgeben*
	suspect	*Verdächtige(r)*
	suspicion	*Verdacht; Misstrauen*

to	**swallow**	*schlucken*
	swamp	*Sumpf*
to	**swear**	*fluchen*
	Sweet as! *(Neuseeländisch, ugs.)*	*Cool!*
to	**swing**	*schwingen*
to	**take a drag**	*(von einer Zigarette) einen Zug nehmen*
to	**take a swing**	*nach jdm. schlagen*
to	**take revenge upon sb.**	*sich an jdm. rächen*
	talkative	*gesprächig*
	tartan	*schottengemustert*
	tea infuser	*Teeei*
to	**tear into sth.**	*sich über etw. hermachen*
	terraced house	*Reihenhaus*
	terrible reputation	*schlechter Ruf*
	terrifying	*furchterregend*
to	**testify**	*aussagen*
to	**text**	*simsen*
	text (message)	*SMS*
	The signal is weak.	*Der Empfang ist schlecht.*
	They were all on top of him.	*Sie fielen alle über ihn her.*
	though	*jedoch*
	threat	*Bedrohung*
	threatening	*bedrohend*
	thud	*dumpfer Schlag*
	thunder	*Donner*
to	**tie**	*festbinden*
	tied to	*angebunden an*
to	**tighten**	*zusammenziehen*
	toast	*Trinksrpuch*
	topic	*Thema*
	torch	*Taschenlampe*
	trace	*Spur*
	track	*Spur*
to	**trap sb.**	*jdn. in die Falle locken*
	trouble	*Ärger*
	troubled	*bekümmert*
	troubling	*beunruhigend*
	trunk *(AE)*	*Kofferraum*
	tube	*Londoner U-Bahn*
to	**tumble**	*fallen*
	twist	*Wendung*
	unbelieving	*ungläubig*
	uncommon	*ungewöhnlich*
	uneasy	*mulmig*
	unkind	*unfreundlich*
	unremarkable	*unscheinbar*
	untidy	*zerstrubbelt*
	upper sixth form	*gymnasiale Oberstufe*
	upset	*traurig; bestürzt*
to	**upset sb.**	*jdn. durcheinander bringen*
	urgently	*dringend*
	vaguely	*annähernd*
	van	*Lieferwagen*
	vengeance	*Rache*
	venom	*Gift*
	verdict	*Urteilsspruch*
	vertical	*senkrecht*
	vibrant	*lebendig*
	victim	*Opfer*
	victorious	*siegreich*
	vigorously	*energisch*
	virtually	*praktisch*
	visible	*sichtbar*
	waist	*Taille*
to	**wake sb. up**	*jdn. wecken*
	warden	*Gefängnisdirektor(in)*
	wardrobe	*Kleiderschrank*
to	**wash over sb.**	*jdn. überschwemmen*
	waste of time	*Zeitverschwendung*
	waterfalls	*Wasserfälle*
	weak	*schwach*
to	**weaken**	*schwächen*
	weapon	*Waffe*
to	**wear**	*tragen*
	weird	*seltsam*
	wet	*nass*
	We would...	*Wir haben immer...*
	What the hell? *(ugs.)*	*Was zum Teufel?*
	wheat	*Weizen*
	whereas	*während*
	whisper	*Flüstern*
to	**whistle**	*pfeifen*

	white lie	*Notlüge*
	width	*Breite*
	wig	*Perücke*
	will	*Testament*
to	**wipe one's hands on sth.**	*sich die Hände an etw. abwischen*
	wire	*Wanze (Abhörgerät)*
	wiseguy *(AE)*	*Gangster von der Mafia*
	witness	*Zeuge/Zeugin*
to	**wonder**	*sich fragen*
	workman	*Handwerker*
to	**worry**	*sich Sorgen machen*
	worse	*schlimmer*
	wounded	*verletzt*
to	**wrap (sth. around sth.)**	*(etw. um etw.) wickeln*
	wrist	*Handgelenk*
	yard	*Hof; Yard (0,914 Meter)*
	You're in for a treat.	*Du kannst dich auf etwas ganz Besonderes freuen.*

BILDQUELLEN

Umschlag:
Akte: Thinkstock/RTimages; Rabe, Friedhof: istock/Thomas_Zsebok_Images; Vollmond, Friedhof: istock/johnnorth

S. 3 (Dominic Butler): Dominic Butler; **S. 6-7 (Weltkarte):** shutterstock/Tetiana Yurchenko; **S. 13 (Stonehenge):** shutterstock/Giancarlo Liguori; **S. 19 (Loch Ness):** shutterstock/Richard Melichar; **S. 26 (Yorkshire Moors):** shutterstock/AC Rider; **S. 33 (Queen Mary the Second):** shutterstock/Shaun Jeffers; **S. 40 (Criminal Court building):** shutterstock/Alex Yeung; **S. 47 (Reihenhäuser):** shutterstock/Andresr; **S. 54 (Route 66):** shutterstock/Nick Fox; **S. 61 (Takakkaw Falls):** shutterstock/Thomas Barrat; **S. 69 (Oxford):** shutterstock/Kamira; **S. 77 (London tube station):** shutterstock/pio3; **S. 85 (Belize):** shutterstock/Anton_Ivanov; **S. 92 (Lancashire):** shutterstock/peter jeffreys; **S. 100 (Houston, Texas):** shutterstock/holbox; **S. 108 (Central Park):** shutterstock/T photography; **S. 116 (Lake District):** shutterstock/Ian Duffield; **S. 123 (Virgin Islands):** shutterstock/Dorn1530; **S. 130 (Northern Territories, Australia):** shutterstock/edella; **S. 138 (Sunnyvale, California):** shutterstock/Andrew Zarivny; **S. 146 (Auckland Prison, New Zealand):** shutterstock/Mati Nitibhon; **S. 153 (The Angel of the North):** shutterstock/Alastair Wallace; **S. 161 (Grand Canyon):** shutterstock/RRuntsch; **S. 168 (Folsom Prison):** shutterstock/Keith McIntyre; **S. 175 (Oil platforms, Cromarty, UK):** shutterstock/ZRyzner; **S. 183 (Fairbanks, Alaska):** shutterstock/Gary Whitton; **S. 191 (Ottawa, Canada):** shutterstock/Click Images; **S. 198 (Royal Albert Hall):** shutterstock/Neil Mitchell; **S. 205 (New Zealand, North Island):** shutterstock/Tupungato; **S. 212 (Statue of Liberty):** shutterstock/T photography; **S. 220 (Sun City, South Africa):** shutterstock/Athol Lewis; **S. 234 (Calais):** shutterstock/David Hughes.